Student Applications Book

Great Source Education Group
a Houghton Mifflin Company
Wilmington, Massachusetts

www.greatsource.com

AUTHORS

Laura Robb
Author

Powhatan School, Boyce, Virginia
Laura Robb, author of *Reading Strategies That Work* and *Teaching Reading in Middle School,* has taught language arts at Powhatan School in Boyce, Virginia, for more than 30 years. She is a co-author of the *Reading and Writing Sourcebooks* for grades 3–5 and the *Summer Success: Reading* program. Robb also mentors and coaches teachers in Virginia public schools and speaks at conferences throughout the country on reading and writing.

Ron Klemp
Contributing Author

Los Angeles Unified School District, Los Angeles, California
Ron Klemp is the Coordinator of Reading for the Los Angeles Unified School District. He has taught Reading, English, and Social Studies and was a middle school Dean of Discipline. He is also a coordinator/facilitator at the Secondary Practitioner Center, a professional development program in the Los Angeles Unified School District. He has been teaching at California State University, Cal Lutheran University, and National University.

Wendell Schwartz
Contributing Author

Adlai Stevenson High School, Lincolnshire, Illinois
Wendell Schwartz has been a teacher of English for 36 years. For the last 24 years he also has served as the Director of Communication Arts at Adlai Stevenson High School. He has taught gifted middle school students for the last 12 years, as well as teaching graduate-level courses for National-Louis University in Evanston, Illinois.

Editorial:
Design:
Illustrations:

Developed by Nieman, Inc.
Ronan Design: Christine Ronan, Sean O'Neill, Maria Mariottini
Mike McConnell

Printed in the United States of America

International Standard Book Number: 0-669-48862-3
(Student Applications Book)

2 3 4 5 6 7 8 9—DBH—08 07 06 05 04 03

International Standard Book Number: 0-669-49083-0
(Student Applications Book, Teacher's Edition)

2 3 4 5 6 7 8 9—DBH—08 07 06 05 04 03

Table of Contents for Student Applications Book

Lessons

What Happens When You Read

Reading is a process. It happens over time—over the course of a few minutes, a few hours, or even a few days if the book is very long or very entertaining. Good readers know how to get "lost" in a book.

Visualizing Reading

An important part of learning to be a better reader is seeing reading for what it really is. How do you visualize yourself reading?

Directions: Draw a picture of yourself reading a really great book. Use "balloons" to show your thoughts.

This is me reading.

Questions for Readers

Every time you pick up a book, you automatically ask yourself a series of questions. Most of the time, this is completely unconscious. But if you actually "listen" to the questions you are asking yourself, it can help you become a better reader.

The questions you ask yourself have to do with why you're reading the book, what you think you'll get out of it, and how long it's going to take to finish.

Directions: Pick out a book that you'd like to read from the classroom library. Then ask yourself these questions about it.

Title:	Author's Name:
What am I reading about?	
Why am I reading?	
What do I want to get out of my reading?	
What kind of reading is it?	
Should I read slowly or quickly?	
How will I know if I've understood the most important ideas?	
How can I remember what I've read?	
Should I reread?	

FOR USE WITH PAGES 32–37

The Reading Process

A reading process is the steps you follow to read, understand, and remember a text.

Your Reading Process

Everyone has his or her own habits and rituals when it comes to reading. What are yours? What do you do before, during, and after reading?

Directions: Describe your own reading process. Make notes or write in full sentences.

Before Reading

....

....

....

....

During Reading

....

....

....

....

After Reading

....

....

....

....

© GREAT SOURCE. ALL RIGHTS RESERVED.

NAME

The Handbook's Reading Process

The handbook's reading process is like a road map you can refer to when reading. Use the "map" to prevent yourself from getting lost. You can use the reading process at school and at home. Some of the steps in the process will be familiar to you, and some will be brand new.

Directions: Skim pages 32–36 of the *Reader's Handbook*. Then retell the reading process as it is described.

Before Reading

....

....

....

....

During Reading

....

....

....

....

After Reading

....

....

....

....

If you get stuck, look at Summing Up on page 37 in your handbook.

NAME ....

FOR USE WITH PAGES 40–42

Reading Know-how

You already have plenty of reading know-how. The key is figuring out how to use it. A first step is to sharpen your essential thinking skills.

Thinking Skill 1: Making Inferences

Making inferences means taking something you read and putting it with something you already know to draw a conclusion.

Directions: Read the paragraph in the box. Then circle the answers that correctly complete the inference statements. Explain what led you to these inferences.

Sample Paragraph

Thirty eighth-graders gather at the local park. They carry trash bags, hoes, rakes, and pruning shears. They divide into groups and make their way to the perimeter of the park. Each group quietly sets to work. There is very little talk besides a couple of the students saying, "Pass me that hoe, please." In the center of the park, a student sets up a water station. Two other students stand at the entrance of the park and distribute fliers that say "You Can Volunteer Too!"

My Inferences

The students are at the park to _____.   clean graffiti   learn about trees   garden

How I know this:

The mood of the group is _____.   angry   determined   festive

How I know this:

The group is _____.   being paid for their work   volunteering their time

How I know this:

Thinking Skill 2: Drawing Conclusions

When you draw conclusions, you put together bits of information and look at the big picture.

Directions: Think again about the thirty kids at the park. Read the facts in the left column. Write your conclusions on the right.

Drawing Conclusions Chart

Facts	Conclusions
Fact 1. Thirty eighth-graders are at a park carrying hoes, rakes, and trash bags.	
Fact 2. A student sets up a water station in the middle of the park.	
Fact 3. There is very little talking except for things like "Pass me that hoe, please."	
Fact 4. Two students distribute "You Can Volunteer Too!" fliers.	

Thinking Skill 3: Comparing and Contrasting

Comparing and contrasting means noticing how things are alike and different.

Directions: Put two school textbooks on your desk. Compare them in terms of size, shape, thickness, and appearance. Write your notes on this Venn Diagram.

Venn Diagram

Write notes that describe Book A here.

Write notes that describe Book B here.

Book A

Both

Book B

Title: ....

Title: ....

Write what they have in common.

Thinking Skill 4: Evaluating

When you evaluate, you make judgments. You tell how you feel about a person, place, thing, or idea; then you explain your opinion.

Directions: Think about two courses you take in school. Tell which you think is more interesting. Then explain why.

I think .... is more interesting than

.... because ....

....

Reading Actively

Active readers notice everything. They ask questions, make predictions, and connect a reading to their own lives.

Ways of Reading Actively

Good readers mark, highlight, and make notes. They react to the author's words and visualize the events described.

Directions: Turn to page 45 in the *Reader's Handbook* and reread "Ways of Reading Actively." Then do an active reading of this paragraph from the book *Farewell to Manzanar.*

from *Farewell to Manzanar* by Jeanne Wakatsuki Houston

1. Mark

Highlight information about time and place.

2. Question

Ask a question about the action here.

The name Manzanar meant nothing to us when we left Boyle Heights. We didn't know where it was or what it was. We went because the government ordered us to. And, in the case of my older brothers and sisters, we went with a certain amount of relief. They had all heard stories of Japanese homes being attacked, of beatings in the streets of California towns. They were as frightened of the Caucasians as Caucasians were of us. Moving, under what appeared to be government protection, to an area less directly threatened by the war seemed not such a bad idea at all. For some it actually sounded like a fine adventure. . . .

We had pulled up just in time for dinner. The mess halls weren't completed

from *Farewell to Manzanar* by Jeanne Wakatsuki Houston, continued

3. React

Explain how the writing makes you feel here.

yet. An outdoor chow line snaked around a half-finished building that broke a good part of the wind. They issued us army mess kits, the round metal kind that fold over, and plopped in scoops of canned Vienna sausage, canned string beans, steamed rice that had been cooked too long, and on top of the rice a serving of canned apricots. The Caucasian servers were thinking that the fruit poured over rice would make a good dessert. Among the Japanese, of course, rice is never eaten with sweet foods, only with salty or savory foods. Few of us could eat such a mixture.

4. Predict

Predict what you think Manzanar is here.

6. Clarify

Write your inferences about the narrator here.

5. Visualize

Make a sketch of the scene here.

Reading Paragraphs

To analyze a paragraph, find the subject first. Then decide what you think the author's message about the subject is. Follow these steps.

Step 1: Read the paragraph.

Your first step is to do an active reading of the paragraph.

Directions: Read this paragraph from an essay by Jorge Luis Borges. Highlight any repeated words. Make notes as you read.

from "Blindness" by Jorge Luis Borges

One of the colors that the blind—or at least this blind man—do *not* see is black; another is red. *Le rouge et le noir* are the colors denied us. I, who was accustomed to sleeping in total darkness, was bothered for a long time at having to sleep in this world of mist, in the greenish or bluish mist, vaguely luminous, which is the world of the blind. I wanted to lie down in darkness. The world of the blind is not the night that people imagine. (I should say that I am speaking for myself, and for my father and my grandmother, who both died blind—blind, laughing, and brave, as I also hope to die. They inherited many things—blindness, for example—but one does not inherit courage. I know that they were brave.)

My question about the main idea of this paragraph:

According to Borges, the world of the blind looks:

Step 2: Find the subject of the paragraph.

To find the subject, ask yourself: "What is this paragraph mostly about?"
You can find the subject by looking at these things:

- the title
- the first sentence
- key words or repeated words or names

Directions: Answer this question about the essay.

What is Jorge Luis Borges mostly talking about in his essay?

....

....

Step 3: Find the main idea of the paragraph.

Implied Main Idea

Often, the main idea of a paragraph is implied. The reader must make inferences about the point the author is trying to make about the subject. That means going through the paragraph sentence by sentence, piecing together the meaning.

Directions: Complete this Main Idea Organizer.

Main Idea Organizer

Subject			
Detail 1	**Detail 2**	**Detail 3**	**Detail 4**
Main Idea			

NAME ....

Reading  History

When you read a history textbook, you need to understand and keep track of the facts, emotions, and ideas described. This reading plan can help.

Before Reading

Use the reading process and the strategy of note-taking to help you read and understand a history chapter on the French and Indian War.

A Set a Purpose

When reading history, your purpose is to find answers to these five questions: *who, what, where, when,* and *why.*

• **Use the 5 W's as your purpose for reading.**

<u>Directions:</u> Ask five questions about the French and Indian War.

My Questions

1. WHO? ....

....

2. WHAT? ....

....

3. WHERE? ....

....

4. WHEN? ....

....

5. WHY? ....

....

B Preview

To preview history, take a look at the chapter's first and last paragraphs and any headings, photos, diagrams, or maps.

Directions: Preview "The French and Indian War." Then return to your five questions and answer as many of them as you can.

from America the Nation

7 The French and Indian War

Study Guide

Main Idea: During the French and Indian War, Great Britain and France fought for control of North America.

Goals: As you read, look for answers to these questions:

1. When did the French and Indian War take place?

2. What role did the Iroquois and other Native American tribes play?

3. What happened at the Battle of Quebec?

Key Terms

allies

exports

confederacy

neutral

alliance

stronghold

Figure 7.1 British-French Conflict, 1689–1763

The French and Indian War (1756–1763) was the last of a series of four North American wars that began in 1689 (see Figure 7.1). In each of these four wars, France and Great Britain fought for control of the territory of North America.

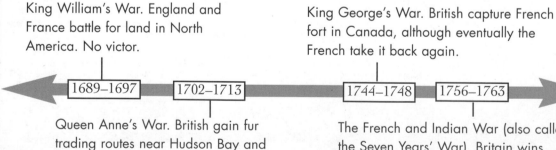

King William's War. England and France battle for land in North America. No victor.

King George's War. British capture French fort in Canada, although eventually the French take it back again.

1689–1697   1702–1713   1744–1748   1756–1763

Queen Anne's War. British gain fur trading routes near Hudson Bay and fishing villages in Nova Scotia.

The French and Indian War (also called the Seven Years' War). Britain wins control of lands in eastern North America.

NAME ....

Textbooks

The French and Indian War, which took place in North America, involved Great Britain and its American colonies against the French and their Iroquois Nation **allies.** Both sides fought with the goal of controlling the continent's valuable **exports,** or products sent abroad for trade or sale. The most valuable of these exports were fur and fish.

Stop and Record

When and where did the French and Indian War take place? Make notes on your 5 W's Organizer (page 21).

Early Struggles

The French and Indian War actually began with a conflict over the Ohio River Valley. For more than a generation, the Iroquois **Confederacy,** a group of several Iroquois nations, had dominated the Ohio Valley. Up to this point, the Iroquois Confederacy had managed to exclude both the French and British from taking hold of the area.

For the most part, the Iroquois tried to stay **neutral,** or not aligned with, either side in the conflict. However, some Iroquois leaders thought it would be wise to form an **alliance,** or political partnership with one side or the other. As a result, many Iroquois began fighting on the side of the French, whom they considered the stronger of the two forces.

The Ohio River Valley

During the 1740s, British traders moved into the Ohio River Valley region and established relationships with Native American tribes who were enemies of the Iroquois. These tribes protected the British traders against Iroquois attack. They also helped the traders build a massive fort at the forks of the Ohio River.

The French were furious that the British had gained a **stronghold,** or fortress, in the Ohio River Valley. Without delay, French troops reinforced their existing forts south of Lake Erie and forced the British to abandon their fort at the forks of the Ohio.

This conflict in the Ohio River Valley marked the official start of the French and Indian War. For the next couple of years, each side attacked enemy forts in unsettled areas along the frontier. However, neither the British nor the French made much progress in their goal to take control of North America.

Stop and Record

Who went to battle in the Ohio River Valley? What role did the Iroquois play? Make notes on your 5 W's Organizer (page 21).

Conflict in Canada

In the third year of the war, British troops began moving toward Canada in an attempt to sweep the French from its shores. A series of bloody battles took place in and around Quebec, the French capital, and within Nova Scotia. Thousands of lives were lost. The French in particular suffered terrible losses.

Wolfe and Montcalm in the Battle of Quebec, French and Indian War. After painting by A. Thoby.

By 1759, it appeared that the British might win the war. Iroquois leaders who had aligned themselves with the French switched sides and began fighting alongside the British. This strengthened the British army considerably and put France firmly on the defensive.

The Battle of Quebec

In 1759, British troops made preparations to attack the fortified city of Quebec, which sat atop a cliff about 180 feet high. At the time, Quebec was defended by more than 14,000 French troops.

On the night of September 12, 1759, 4,500 British troops secretly climbed the steep cliffs that surrounded Quebec. When the French soldiers guarding Quebec woke the next morning, they saw the British troops standing with their guns held high.

The French soldiers, some of whom were untrained, had little idea how to handle this British invasion. They shot wildly at the British troops and watched in despair as the British moved toward them. The well-trained British soldiers moved closer and closer to the French, firing as they marched. One French soldier after another fell to the ground. Within thirty minutes, the battle was over. The British had won Quebec and the key to power over most of North America.

Stop and Record

Why did both France and Britain want control of North America? Make notes on your 5 W's Organizer (page 21).

C Plan

You probably found some answers to your 5 W's questions on your preview.
When you do your careful reading, watch for additional facts and details.
Take notes as you go.

• Use a 5 W's Organizer to keep track of what you learn.

During Reading

D Read with a Purpose

Keep your purpose in mind as you read. You are looking for answers to *who*,
what, *where*, *when*, and *why*.

Directions: Write your During Reading notes on the 5 W's Organizer below.
Be as detailed as possible.

5 W's Organizer

Subject				
Who	**What**	**Where**	**When**	**Why**

Textbooks

Using the Strategy

There are many types of organizers you can use to keep track of important facts as you read. Choose the one that works best for you, or the one that you think will work best with the text.

- **Paragraph-by-Paragraph notes can help you keep track of the most important facts.**

Directions: Return to the chapter. Find the most important fact from each of the first five paragraphs. Write it on the chart below.

Paragraph-by-Paragraph Notes

Paragraph #	Most Important Fact
1	France and Britain fought a series of four wars over territory in North America.
2	
3	
4	
5	

Understanding How
History Textbooks Are Organized

Most history chapters open with a study guide or "goals" box. Take the time to learn the information in this box.

Directions: Return to the study guide on page 18. Then answer the questions and define the terms.

Questions

1. When did the French and Indian War take place?

....

....

2. What role did the Iroquois and other Native American tribes play?

....

....

....

....

3. What happened at the Battle of Quebec?

....

....

....

....

....

Key Terms

allies ....

exports ....

confederacy ....

neutral ....

alliance ....

stronghold ....

Textbooks

E Connect

Making a personal connection to what you're reading can make history "come alive."

- **Imagining yourself a part of history can help you make a strong connection to the text.**

Directions: Put yourself in an Iroquois leader's place during this period.

How would you have felt about the French and British?

....

....

....

At this point, take a moment to consider what you've learned.

 F Pause and Reflect

Return to your 5 W's Organizer. Ask yourself "Have I answered each of the five questions to my satisfaction?"

- **After you finish a selection, decide whether you've met your purpose.**

Directions: Answer these two questions about the history chapter.

1. Which parts did you find easiest to understand?

....

2. Which were most challenging? Why?

....

....

 G Reread

Use a rereading tool. Make an Outline to keep track of the most important facts and details in a selection.

- **At the rereading stage, create an Outline of the chapter or article.**

NAME ....

Directions: Complete this Outline. Refer to your notes and the reading. Use the article or chapter headings as major divisions in your Outline.

◀ **Outline** ▶

I. Early Struggles

A. Detail

....

....

B. Detail

....

....

II. The Ohio River Valley

A. Detail

....

....

B. Detail

....

....

III.

A. Detail

....

....

B. Detail

....

....

IV.

A. Detail

....

....

B. Detail

....

Textbooks

Remember

Choose a tool that can help you remember what you learned in the history chapter.

• **Sharing information with others can help you remember it.**

<u>Directions:</u> Write three facts about the French and Indian War to share with a classmate.

◄ **Important Facts**

1. ....

....

....

2. ....

....

....

3. ....

....

....

Reading Geography

If you're struggling with geography, it might be because of how you're reading the textbook. Practice reading and responding to a geography text here.

Before Reading

On these pages, you'll use the reading process and the strategy of using graphic organizers to help you read and respond to a geography chapter. Take what you learn here and apply it to your own reading.

 A Set a Purpose

Your purpose for reading a geography chapter is twofold. First, you need to find out the subject of the chapter. Next, you need to learn why the information is important.

• **To set your purpose, turn the title of the geography chapter into a question.**

Directions: Write your purpose for reading this excerpt from a textbook chapter called "The Mountains of Canada and the United States." Then write two prereading questions.

My purpose: ....

....

....

My prereading questions: ....

....

....

 B Preview

Previewing helps you know what to expect during your close reading.

Directions: Preview the geography chapter. Write on the sticky notes.

7 The Mountains of Canada and the United States

Preview

Key Terms

plains
tectonic plates
intermontane
plateaus
mesas
lowlands

Places to Locate

the Pacific Ranges
the Interior and Great
    Plains
the Rocky Mountains
the Appalachian
    Mountains

Read and Learn—

1. land forms of the
    United States and
    Canada
2. water sources of the
    United States and
    Canada

Canada and the United States both are located on the continent of North America. Together, these two nations cover more than 7 million square miles (see Figure 7.1) and share basically the same land forms.

Geographers call the United States and Canada a land of mountains and **plains,** which are extensive, level, and relatively treeless areas of land. Both countries have huge, snowcapped mountains in the west, grassy plains in the center, and low, rolling mountains in the east. Among the most famous features are the Rocky Mountains, the Great Plains, the Appalachian Mountains, and the Canadian Shield.

I noticed this about the graphics:

_____

_____

_____

_____

_____

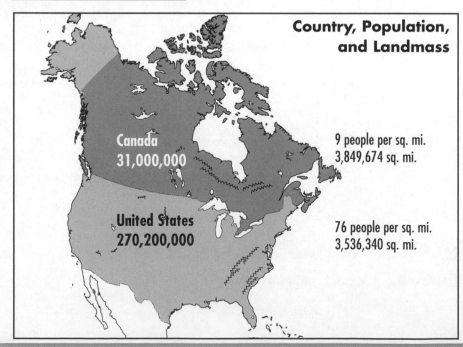

Country, Population, and Landmass

Canada
31,000,000

9 people per sq. mi.
3,849,674 sq. mi.

United States
270,200,000

76 people per sq. mi.
3,536,340 sq. mi.

Figure 7.1
Country Profiles

Western Mountain Ranges

The western mountain ranges in Canada and the United States are among the most magnificent in the world. These ranges, which parallel the Pacific Ocean, were formed by the collision of two **tectonic plates,** or large pieces of the earth's crust. This event occurred over time millions of years ago. The result of the clashing is a mountain system called the Pacific Ranges. It includes the Alaska Range, the Coast Ranges, the Cascade Range, and the mighty Sierra Nevada.

East of the Pacific Ranges lies another enormous mountain range, called the Rocky Mountains. The Rocky Mountains extend more than three thousand miles, from northern Alaska to northern New Mexico. The Rockies also were formed by tectonic forces millions of years ago. The tallest part of the Rockies is in the state of Colorado. Here, the Rockies' mountainous peaks are more than 14,000 feet high.

The Intermontane

The area that lies between the Rockies and the Pacific Ranges is known as the **intermontane** (meaning "between two mountains or ranges"). This is an area of basins and plateaus. The **plateaus,** which are high, level surfaces, lie in the northern and southern areas between the two ranges. **(see Figures 7.2)**

The most notable of the plateaus is the Colorado Plateau, which has eroded over time. The results of this erosion are the magnificent Grand Canyon and several flat-topped areas of land known as **mesas.**

Eastern Mountains and Lowlands

On the eastern side of North America lie the Appalachian Mountains. This mountain range, which is the second largest in North America, is 1,500 miles long and extends from the Canadian province of Quebec to Alabama in the United States.

The subject of the chapter is:

The first paragraph tells me:

Key terms to learn are:

Textbooks

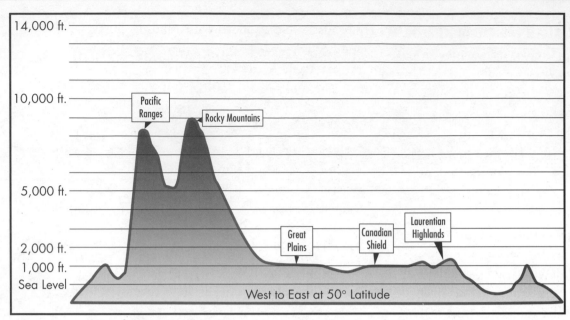

Figure 7.2 Elevation Profile of Canada

Figure 7.3 Elevation Profile of the United States

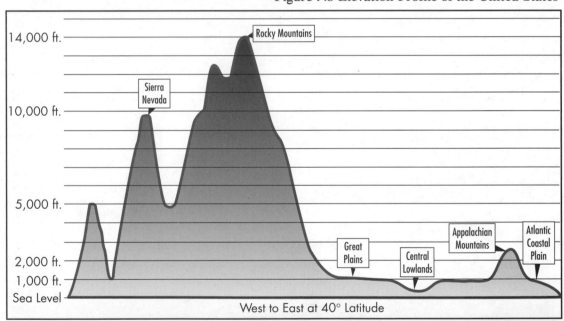

Questions
What is the tallest mountain range in the United States and Canada?
What area in the United States is bordered by the Atlantic Ocean?

To the east and the south of the Appalachians in the United States is an area known as the coastal **lowlands.** Lowlands are similar to valleys in that they lie lower than surrounding areas.

The Piedmont, the Atlantic Coastal Plain, and the Gulf Coastal Plain are all a part of this lowland area. **(see Figures 7.2 and 7.3)**

C Plan

Next, choose a strategy that can help you meet your reading purpose.

• Use graphic organizers to keep track of important information.

Directions: Make notes on this K-W-L Chart. Write what you already know about the geography of Canada and the United States in Column 1. Write what you want to learn in Column 2. Save Column 3 for later.

K-W-L Chart

What I **K**now	What I **W**ant to Know	What I **L**earned

During Reading

Now go back and do a careful reading of the geography chapter. Write important facts and details in Column 3 of your organizer.

D Read with a Purpose

Remember to keep your purpose in mind as you read. Your goal is to find out what the chapter is about and why this information is important.

Using the Strategy

Many different kinds of graphic organizers work well with geography textbooks. Choose the organizer that works best for you, or the one that you think will work best with the reading.

- **A Concept Map can help you explore important terms and ideas in the reading.**

Directions: Write important facts and details about mountain ranges on this Concept Map.

Concept Map

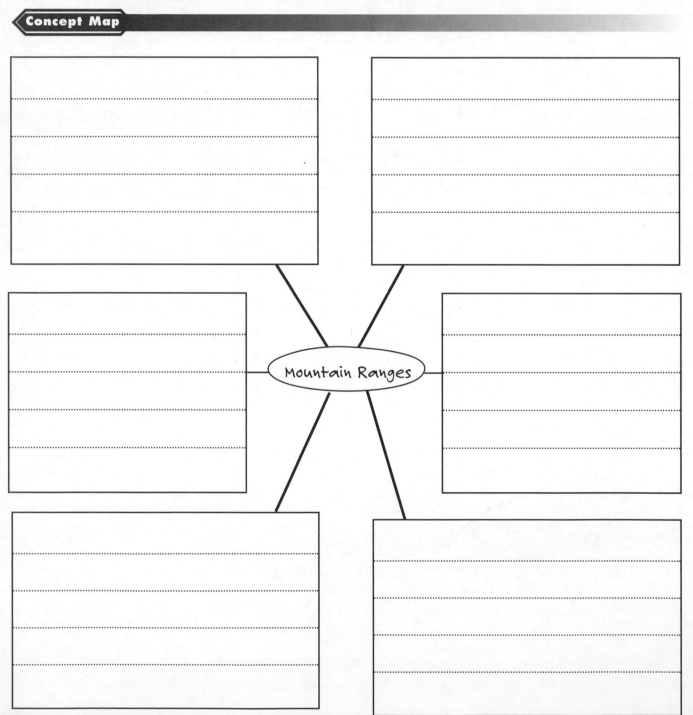

Understanding How
Geography Textbooks Are Organized

Geography textbooks are organized around **topics** and **graphics.**

1. Topic Organization In most geography chapters, you'll find several key topics. Within each topic there may be two or more subtopics.

Directions: Look at the sample Outline on page 94 of your handbook. Then complete this Outline using notes from the reading.

Textbooks

◆ **Outline**

I. Western Mountain Ranges ....

    A. Subpoint ....

    B. Subpoint ....

    C. Subpoint ....

II. The Intermontane ....

    A. Subpoint ....

    B. Subpoint ....

    C. Subpoint ....

III. Eastern Mountains and Lowlands ....

    A. Subpoint ....

    B. Subpoint ....

2. Graphics Organization In addition to paying attention to key topics, you must also look carefully at the maps, graphs, tables, and photographs that appear throughout the chapter.

Directions: Look at the map on page 28. Write one sentence that summarizes it. Then do the same for the elevation profiles on page 30.

One-sentence Summary

Map:

Elevation Profiles:

Connect

Making personal connections to a geography text can help you understand and stay interested in what you're reading.

- **As you read, make notes about information that you find interesting, surprising, or puzzling.**

<u>Directions:</u> Record your connections to the geography chapter here.

My Connections

I was interested in these parts of the reading:

....

....

I found this information surprising:

....

....

I'm puzzled by this:

....

....

After Reading

After you finish reading, take the time to consider what you've learned.

 Pause and Reflect

Begin by reflecting on your reading purpose.

- **Ask yourself, "How well did I meet my purpose?"**

<u>Directions:</u> Return to the Column 3 of your K-W-L Chart (page 31). Make notes about what you learned. Circle *have* or *have not* to show whether you've met your reading purpose. Explain.

I have / have not met my reading purpose. Here's why:

....

....

....

....

Reread

Even the best readers can take in and retain only so much on a first reading. For this reason, it's a good idea to look back and reread.

• A powerful rereading strategy to use with geography is note-taking.

Directions: Reread the excerpt. Write a question about the mountains of Canada and the United States on the front of each Study Card. Then, exchange books with a classmate, and have him or her answer the questions.

Textbooks

Study Cards

Question:

Question:

Answer:

Answer:

NAME ....

FOR USE WITH PAGES 84–99

 Remember

It's vital that you figure out a way to remember what you've learned.

• **Creating a practice test can help you remember important facts and details from a geography reading.**

Directions: Create a practice test about the geography chapter. Then turn the book upside-down and make an answer key.

1. What is a plateau

    a. A small bridge   b.

    c.   d.

2.

    a.   b.

    c.   d.

3.

    a.   b.

    c.   d.

4.

    a.   b.

    c.   d.

5.

    a.   b.

    c.   d.

Answer Key

Reading Science

Good scientists are good readers. They know strategies that can help them get more from every article, chapter, and book they read. Practice reading and responding to a science textbook here.

Before Reading

Use the reading process and the strategy of note-taking to help you read and understand science textbook pages about light and refraction.

A Set a Purpose

Your purpose when reading science is to find out as much as you can about the subject. Another part of your purpose is to understand why the subject is important.

• To set your purpose, ask a question about the subject and main idea.

Directions: Write your purpose for reading "Understanding Light" here. Then make a prediction. What do you expect to learn?

My purpose: ....

....

Here are three things I expect to learn: ....

1. ....

....

2. ....

....

3. ....

....

Textbooks

NAME ....

B Preview

The title can give you your first clue about the subject of the material.
Previewing the features on the checklist below will provide additional clues.

Preview Checklist

☐ headings

☐ any boxed items

☐ any repeated words or terms in boldface

☐ any photos, maps, graphs, or diagrams

Directions: Skim the two science pages that follow. Place a check mark
beside each feature as you preview it. Then make notes on the preview
chart.

Preview Chart

The titles and headings tell me . . .	I noticed these repeated words . . .

(Understanding Light)

The graphics tell me . . .	I expect to learn . . .

SECTION

3 Understanding Light

DISCOVER

1. Learn the chief characteristics of light.
2. Explore how light travels.
3. Understand the laws of refraction.

RESEARCH

• Check your library or do an Internet search for information on mirages. Learn what causes them and what they have to do with refracted light.

GOALS

1. Find out about reflection.
2. Understand the color spectrum.

Key Terms
radiates
photons
oblique
refraction
angle of incidence

Tip for Reading As you read, make a list of the characteristics of light. Use this list to help you understand qualities of reflection and refraction.

Light Facts
• The study of light and how it behaves is called optics.
• Ordinary white light is made up of a spectrum, or range, of colors: red, orange, yellow, green, blue, indigo, and violet.
• White is the mixture of all colors of light. Black indicates all colors are absorbed.
• In empty space, light travels at the speed of 186,282 miles per second.

Light is a form of electromagnetic energy that can be detected by the human eye. Without it, we could not see. Light **radiates,** or travels in straight lines in all directions, from its source. It is made up of tiny particles called **photons.**

Anything that gives off light is called a light source. The sun is earth's primary light source, although humans have many artificial light sources, including electric lights, flashlights, candles, and so on.

Measuring the Speed of Light

Light waves travel faster through air than through water, glass, or other materials. The speed of light in a vacuum is a fundamental physical constant. The currently accepted value of the speed of light is 299,792,458 meters per second, or about 186,282 miles per second.

Reflection and Refraction

No matter what its source, light travels only in straight lines. We can see objects around us because they reflect, or bounce, light into our eyes. Light-colored surfaces, such as a piece of glass, reflect more light than dark surfaces. When light is reflected, it still travels in straight lines.

When a light ray passes at an **oblique,** or sloping, angle from one material to another, its path appears to bend. This is called **refraction.** In refraction, the light ray only appears to bend **(see Figure 3.1).** Refracted light, like reflected light, also travels in straight lines.

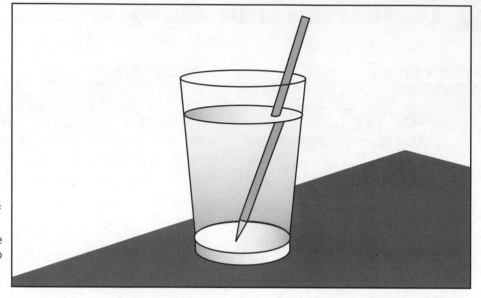

**Figure 3.1:
Refraction** This
pencil in a glass of
water seems to
bend at the surface
of the water due to
refraction.

The Law of Reflection

Light travels through space in what are called **rays of light**. It's
possible to change the direction of a ray through reflection. For example, a
mirror or any other shiny surface can reflect light. With a plane, or flat-
faced, mirror, light is reflected at an angle equal to the angle at which the
ray hits the mirror. This is called the **angle of incidence** and can be written
as a mathematical formula:

$$<I=<R$$

The angle of incidence (I) is equal to the angle of reflection (R).

**Figure 3.2: The
Angle of Incidence**
Light is reflected at
an angle equal to
the angle at which
it hits the mirror.

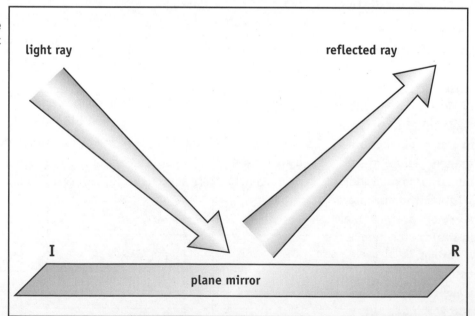

light ray   reflected ray

I   R

plane mirror

C Plan

After previewing a science text, make your plan. Choose a strategy that can help you read, understand, and remember what you've learned.

• Use the strategy of note-taking to get more from a science text.

Before you begin reading, create a Thinking Tree. Use it to keep track of important facts and details from the reading.

During Reading

As you read, make notes on the Thinking Tree. Use the headings from the article as your guide to what's important.

D Read with a Purpose

Remember that your purpose is to discover the subject and main idea of the article.

<u>Directions:</u> Look at the sample Thinking Tree on page 107 of your handbook. Then use the Thinking Tree below for your notes from "Understanding Light."

Thinking Tree

```
┌─────────────────────────────────────────┐
│  Understanding Light                      │
│                                           │
└─────────────────────────────────────────┘
        ┌──────────────────┴──────────────────┐
┌───────────────────────┐        ┌───────────────────────┐
│ Measuring the Speed    │        │ Reflection and         │
│ of Light               │        │ Refraction             │
└───────────────────────┘        └───────────────────────┘
    ┌──────┴──────┐                   ┌──────┴──────┐
┌────────┐  ┌────────┐          ┌────────┐  ┌────────┐
│Detail: │  │Detail: │          │Detail: │  │Detail: │
│        │  │        │          │        │  │        │
└────────┘  └────────┘          └────────┘  └────────┘
```

NAME ....

Using the Strategy

There are many different ways to take notes when reading science. Choose the method that's best for you. For example, you might decide to make Key Word Notes as you work your way through a chapter.

• **Use Key Word Notes to help you learn and remember key concepts in a reading.**

Directions: Complete the Key Word Notes.

Key Word Notes

Key Words	Text Notes
optics	
refraction	
angle of incidence	

Understanding How Science Texts Are Organized

Scientists often think in terms of causes and effects. Many science textbooks are organized around this concept.

Directions: Reread the information about refracted light. Then make notes on this diagram.

Cause and Effect Order

The Law of Reflection

Cause

> Light ray hits a flat, shiny surface.

Effect

E Connect

Good readers ask themselves, "How does this information relate to me?"

- **As you read, make notes about facts and details that you find interesting or puzzling.**

Directions: Write your reactions to "Understanding Light" here. What did you find surprising or interesting? What would you like to learn more about?

My reactions: ....

....

....

....

After Reading

When you finish reading, think about what you've learned.

F Pause and Reflect

Return to your reading purpose. Do you understand the subject and the main idea?

> • **After you finish a chapter, consider whether you've met your purpose.**

Directions: Answer *yes* or *no* to these questions. Remember that you asked a question about the subject and the main idea when you set your purpose.

Purpose Questions

1. Do you know the subject of the article?

_____

2. Do you understand the main point the writer is making about the subject?

_____

3. Can you explain the key terms?

_____

4. Do the graphics, pictures, and captions make sense?

_____

Reread

If you can't answer *yes* to each question, you probably need to do some rereading.

• **Use the strategy of skimming to help you answer specific questions.**

Directions: Skim the excerpt for information that explains angle of incidence. Complete the Thinking Tree.

Thinking Tree

Understanding Light

Subhead:

Angle of Incidence:

 Remember

There's more to science than what you find in your textbook. Make the information your own by talking about it with someone else.

• **Talking about a subject can help you remember it.**

Directions: Interview a family member about light. Write at least two interview questions beforehand.

Interview

Question #1:

Answer:

Question #2:

Answer:

Textbooks

Reading Math

To succeed in math, you must know how to read carefully, think critically, and apply what you've learned. Practice here.

Before Reading

Use the reading process and the strategy of visualizing and thinking aloud to help you read and respond to a grade 8 math text.

A   Set a Purpose

Your first step is to establish your purpose for reading.

- **To set your purpose, turn the title of the chapter or page into a question.**

Directions: Write your purpose for reading "Percents, Fractions, and Decimals." Then tell what you already know about the subject. Finish by explaining what you think will be easiest and hardest about these pages.

My purpose question: ....

....

....

....

What I already know about the subject: ....

....

....

....

What I think will be easiest and hardest: ....

....

....

....

B Preview

Always preview a math assignment before you begin reading. Your preview can help you figure out what you know and what you need to learn.

• **Keep track of your preview notes on a K-W-L Chart.**

<u>Directions:</u> Preview the math page that follows. Pay attention to headings, boxed items, and examples. Make some notes on this K-W-L Chart.

K-W-L Chart for Percents, Fractions, and Decimals

What I **K**now	What I **W**ant to Know	What I **L**earned

| Write what you already know here. | Write what you need to find out about the subject here. | Make notes in this section during your careful reading. |

1.7

This page teaches me

how to ....

....

Percents, Fractions, and Decimals

1. Changing Fractions to Decimals and Percents

To change a fraction to a **decimal,** divide the numerator by the denominator. For example:

$$\frac{5}{10} = 5 \div 10 \text{ and } 5 \div 10 = .5$$

The word **percent** means "per hundred." The symbol for percent is %. To write a fraction as a percent, first rewrite it as a fraction with a denominator of 100. Then divide the numerator by the denominator. For example:

$$\frac{1}{2} = 50/100 = 50 \div 100 = 0.5$$

Decimals can be written as percents. Multiply the decimal by 100.

➼ Example

$$0.5 \times 100 = 50\%$$

$\frac{1}{2}$ apple = 50/100 $\frac{1}{2}$ apple = 0.50 $\frac{1}{2}$ apple = 50%

➼ Additional Examples

$6/10 = 60/100 = 0.6 = 60\%$ $2/5 = 40/100 = 0.4 = 40\%$

Double-check ✔✔ Apply What You've Learned

1. Rewrite the fraction so that its denominator is 100.
   a. $\frac{1}{2}$ b. $\frac{1}{50}$ c. $\frac{4}{5}$ d. $\frac{3}{10}$

2. Write the number as a fraction and as a decimal.
   a. forty-five hundredths
   b. twelve hundredths

A denominator is ....

....

....

....

A numerator is ....

....

....

....

 **Plan**

Most math books are full of information. Choose a strategy that can help you understand and apply the information you read about.

• Use the strategy of visualizing and thinking aloud to help you solve math problems and memorize rules and formulas.

During Reading

Thinking aloud means talking yourself through a problem. It can be as simple as saying, "First I do this, next I do that, and finally I do this other thing to arrive at the answer."

D Read with a Purpose

Now go back and do a careful reading of the math page. Keep your purpose in mind as you read. Write on the sticky notes.

Using the Strategy

Directions: On the lines below, write a Think Aloud that explains how to rewrite a fraction as a percent. Give a sample problem. Draw or sketch to visualize your problem.

Think Aloud

Writing a Fraction as a Percent

....

....

....

....

Visualizing

NAME ....

FOR USE WITH PAGES 117–131

Understanding How
Math Texts Are Organized

Most math chapters have an opening explanation, sample problems, and exercises. Find these three parts on the second page of a math chapter.

This is the

These are

These are

2. Changing Percents to Fractions and Decimals

Knowing how to change percents to fractions and decimals will help you understand information you need to solve many real-life problems. For example, our money system uses decimals. If you have a dollar, it's equal to 100 pennies, or you might write a check for $15.75.

⬥ Example

Suppose that 70 percent of your class eats in the cafeteria. How would you show that percent as a fraction? How would you show it as a decimal?

Solution

To change a percent to a fraction, remove the % sign. Write a fraction with the % as the numerator and 100 as the denominator. Reduce the fraction, if needed. For example:

$$70\% = 70/100 = 7/10$$

To change a percent to a decimal, divide the % by 100. For example:

$$70\% = 70 \div 100 = 0.70$$

Double-check ✔✔ Apply What You've Learned

1. Rewrite the percent as a fraction. Reduce the fraction, if needed.
   a. 85%   b. 15%   c. 2%   d. 63%
2. Rewrite the percent as a decimal.
   a. 5%   b. 30%   c. 49%   d. 54%

Communicating about Mathematics

Directions: Answer these questions.

1. What is a percent? ....

2. What is one reason for learning how to write percents, fractions, and decimals?

....

E Connect

You can make math concepts more interesting and easier to remember if you relate them to your own life. This is called making an "analogy."

• Making an analogy can help you make a connection to the math problem or formula.

Directions: Read the problem and sample analogy. Then create an analogy for Problem 2. Use an event or experience from your own life.

◄ Think Aloud

Problem	Analogy
1. What fraction is equal to 50%?	If my mother gives me fifty percent of a pie, it means that she has given me half. So 50% = 1/2.
2. Write one-fourth as a percent.	

After Reading

At this point, take a moment to reflect on what you've learned.

F Pause and Reflect

Return to your reading purpose. Ask yourself what you've learned about percents, fractions, and decimals.

• When you finish reading, ask yourself, "Did I meet my purpose?"

Directions: Check *yes* or *no* in response to each question.

Checklist	Yes	No
I understand the key terms from the reading.		
I can explain what each term means.		
I understand the sample problems.		
I can take what I've learned and use it to solve the exercises.		

G Reread

It's a good idea to think and rethink the math rules and strategies you've learned. Return to the parts of the text that you're not sure of and do some rereading.

• **A powerful rereading strategy to use is note-taking.**

Directions: Read the concepts in the left column. Write an explanation for each concept in the middle column and an example on the right. One has been done for you.

Key Word Notes

Key Concepts	Explanation	Examples
Writing a fraction as a percent	Rewrite the fraction as a fraction with a denominator of 100. Divide the numerator by the denominator. Multiply the decimal by 100.	$\frac{1}{10} = \frac{10}{100}$ $10 \div 100 = 0.1$ $0.1 \times 100 = 10\%$
Writing a decimal as a percent		
Writing a percent as a fraction		
Writing a percent as a decimal		

H Remember

Usually, new math concepts you learn hinge on concepts you studied previously. For this reason, you must find a way to remember what you've learned.

• **Creating sample tests can help you remember important information.**

Directions: Create a sample test that explores what you learned in the "Percents, Fractions, and Decimals" reading. Give the test to a classmate and see how well he or she does. Then, turn the book upside-down and make an answer key.

Sample Test

Textbooks

Focus on Science Concepts

In science and other subjects, concept *is a word for "big idea." Follow these steps to understand a science concept.*

Step 1: Learn key terms.

An important part of understanding science concepts is learning the definitions for key terms.

Directions: Look at the oxygen cycle diagram below. Write key terms in the word bank. Use a dictionary to define each term.

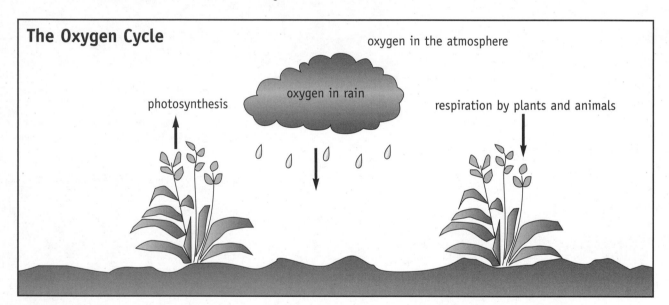

The Oxygen Cycle

oxygen in the atmosphere

photosynthesis

oxygen in rain

respiration by plants and animals

Word Bank

Step 2: Understand the steps in the process.

Your next step is to understand what's involved in the process. Making a Concept Map can help.

Directions: Write the steps of the oxygen cycle here. Include key terms from your word bank.

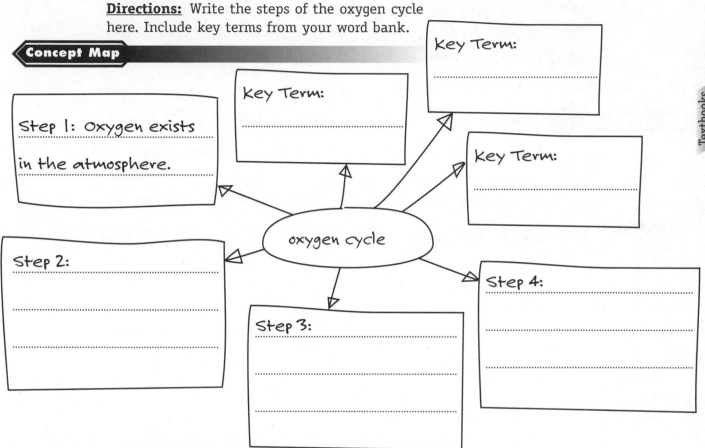

Concept Map

Step 1: Oxygen exists in the atmosphere.

Key Term:

Key Term:

Key Term:

oxygen cycle

Step 2:

Step 3:

Step 4:

Step 3: Redraw or retell.

To make sure you fully understand a concept, explain it in your own words. Redraw the concept or tell what it's all about.

Directions: Look at the redrawing of cell division on page 140 of the *Reader's Handbook*. Then redraw the oxygen cycle in a similar way.

Drawing

Focus on Word Problems

Word problems can be tricky, but they're never impossible. In fact, most word problems are solved in basically the same way. Use this four-step plan.

Step 1: Read.

Begin by reading the problem at least twice. Figure out what it is asking for.

Directions: Read this word problem. Take notes on the "topic," the "given," and the "unknown." Reread page 144 of your handbook if you need help.

Notes

1. Mrs. Devlin's class held a donut sale before school. They sold a total of 200 donuts, which was 10% less than what they had hoped to sell. How many donuts had they hoped to sell?	**Topic** (What the problem is about): **Given** (Important information about the topic): **Unknown** (What you need to find out):

Step 2: Plan.

Next, choose a strategy that will help you solve the problem. The best strategy to use with word problems is visualizing.

Directions: Make a sketch that shows the donut sale problem.

Sketch

Donut Sale

NAME ....

Step 3: Solve.

Use your notes and sketch to help you write a numerical expression.

Directions: Write a numerical expression for the donut sale problem. Then solve the problem.

My expression: ....

....

Step 4: Check.

Always check your work. The strategy of thinking aloud can help.

Directions: Write a Think Aloud that shows how you solved the problem.

◄ **My Think Aloud** ►

I need to find out how many total donuts Mrs. Devlin's class hoped to sell, so I

....

....

....

....

....

....

....

....

....

....

....

....

Reading an Essay

*Essays can be lighthearted or serious, formal or informal.
They can be quick and easy or long and challenging.
As a critical reader, your job is to find out what the
essay is about and then decide what it means.*

Before Reading

You can practice reading and responding to an essay here. Use the reading
process and the strategy of outlining to help you read the essay "Vesuvius"
by Pliny the Younger.

A   Set a Purpose

Setting your purpose before you read can help you understand what
the author is saying about the subject and how you feel about the
author's message.

• **Ask a question about the essay title, the author, or both.**

Directions: Write your purpose for reading Pliny the Younger's essay
"Vesuvius" below.

My purpose: ....

....

....

....

....

....

....

B Preview

Spend the next few minutes previewing. Look at the title and author, first and last paragraphs, and any background information. Also notice the opening quote and any repeated words or phrases.

Directions: Preview "Vesuvius." Write your preview notes on this Web. Add more boxes if you need to.

Web

Author's name:

Essay subject:

Repeated words:

"Vesuvius"

Background information:

Last paragraph details:

First paragraph details:

Nonfiction

from "Vesuvius" by Pliny the Younger

The eruption of Mt. Vesuvius in A.D. 79 destroyed Pompeii and Herculaneum. At the time of the eruption, the Roman fleet, which was under the command of a man named Pliny the Elder, was stationed nearby. When he spotted the "fire in the sky," Pliny the Elder set sail toward the erupting volcano. He wanted to observe what was happening and offer his services if rescues were needed. As it turned out rescues were not possible, and Pliny himself was killed in the confusion.

Pliny's nephew, known as Pliny the Younger, observed the eruption from afar. Afterward, he wrote about the event. Pliny the Younger's writings are considered the first vivid description of a volcanic eruption. In the selection that follows, he refers to Campania, an ancient province in Italy, and to Misenum, an ancient city and Roman naval station.

> "The mind shudders to remember . . .
> but here is the tale."
> —Pliny the Younger

After my uncle's departure I finished up my studies, as I had planned. Then I had a bath, then dinner and a short and unsatisfactory night. There had been tremors for many days previously, a common occurrence in Campania and no cause for panic. But that night the shaking grew much stronger; people thought it was an upheaval, not just a tremor. My mother burst into my room and I got up. I said she should rest, and I would rouse her if need be. We sat out on a small terrace between the house and the sea. I sent for a volume of Livy; I read and even took notes from where I had left off, as if it were a moment of free time; I hardly know whether to call it bravery, or foolhardiness (I was seventeen at the time). Up comes a friend of my uncle's, recently arrived from Spain. When he sees my mother and me sitting there, and me even reading a book, he scolds her for her calm and me for my lack of concern. But I kept on with my book.

Now the day begins, with a still hesitant and almost lazy dawn. All around us buildings are shaken. We are in the open, but it is only a small area and we are afraid, nay certain, that there will be a collapse. We decided to leave the town finally; a dazed crowd follows us, preferring our plan to their own (this is what passes for wisdom in a panic). Their numbers are so large that they slow our departure, and then sweep us along. We stopped once we had left the buildings behind us. Many strange things happened to us there, and we had much to fear.

Stop and Organize
Make some notes in the "Introduction" section of the Outline (page 63).

from "Vesuvius" by Pliny the Younger

The carts that we had ordered brought were moving in opposite directions, though the ground was perfectly flat, and they wouldn't stay in place even with their wheels blocked by stones. In addition, it seemed as though the sea was being sucked backwards, as if it were being pushed back by the shaking of the land. Certainly the shoreline moved outwards, and many sea creatures were left on dry sand. Behind us were frightening dark clouds, rent by lightning twisted and hurled, opening to reveal huge figures of flame. These were like lightning, but bigger. At that point the Spanish friend urged us strongly: "If your brother and uncle is alive, he wants you to be safe. If he has perished, he wanted you to survive him. So why are you reluctant to escape?" We responded that we would not look to our own safety as long as we were uncertain about his. Waiting no longer, he took himself off from the danger at a mad pace. It wasn't long thereafter that the cloud stretched down to the ground and covered the sea. It girdled Capri and made it vanish, it hid Misenum's promontory. Then my mother began to beg and urge and order me to flee however I might, saying that a young man could make it, that she, weighed down in years and body, would die happy if she escaped being the cause of my death. I replied that I wouldn't save myself without her, and then I took her hand and made her walk a little faster. She obeyed with difficulty, and blamed herself for delaying me.

Now came the dust, though still thinly. I look back: a dense cloud looms behind us, following us like a flood poured across the land. "Let us turn aside while we can still see, lest we be knocked over in the street and crushed by the crowd of our companions." We had scarcely sat down when a darkness came that was not like a moonless or cloudy night, but more like the black of closed and unlighted rooms. You could hear women lamenting, children crying, men shouting. Some were calling for parents, others for children or spouses; they could only recognize them by their voices. Some bemoaned their own lot, others that of their near and dear. There were some so afraid of death that they prayed for death. Many raised their hands to the gods, and even more believed that there were no gods any longer and that this was one last unending night for the world. Nor were we without people who magnified real dangers with fictitious horrors. Some announced that one or another part of Misenum had collapsed or burned; lies, but they found believers. It grew lighter, though that seemed not a return of day, but a sign that the fire was approaching. The fire itself actually stopped some distance away, but darkness and ashes came again, a great weight of them. We stood up and shook the ash off again and again, otherwise we would have been covered with it and crushed by the weight. I might boast that no groan escaped me in such perils, no cowardly word, but that I believed that I was perishing with the world, and the world with me, which was a great consolation for death.

Stop and Organize

Make some notes in the "Body" section of the Outline (page 63).

from "Vesuvius" by Pliny the Younger

At last the cloud thinned out and dwindled to no more than smoke or fog. Soon there was real daylight. The sun was even shining, though with the lurid glow it has after an eclipse. The sight that met our still terrified eyes was a changed world, buried in ash like snow. We returned to Misenum and took care of our bodily needs, but spent the night dangling between hope and fear. Fear was the stronger, for the earth was still quaking and a number of people who had gone mad were mocking the evils that had happened to them and others with terrifying prognostications. We still refused to go until we heard news of my uncle, although we had felt danger and expected more.

Stop and Organize
Make some notes in the "Conclusion" section of the Outline (page 63).

C Plan

After your preview, make a plan for reading. How can you best meet your purpose? The strategy of outlining can help.

• **Use the strategy of outlining to make notes as you read an essay.**

During Reading

Watch for the three major parts of the essay: the introduction, the body, and the conclusion.

D Read with a Purpose

Also keep in mind your purpose as you read. Remember that you want to find out what the author is saying about the subject and how you feel about what's being said.

Directions: Do a careful reading of Pliny the Younger's essay. Make notes on this Outline as you read.

Outline

I. Introduction _____

A. Detail: ....

B. Detail: ....

C. Thesis statement: ....

....

II. Body _____

A. Support for thesis: ....

B. Support for thesis: ....

....

C. Support for thesis: ....

....

III. Conclusion _____

A. Concluding detail: ....

B. Concluding detail: ....

C. Concluding detail: ....

Nonfiction

Using the Strategy

To complete your Outline, you must find the main point of the essay. Use this formula to help:

subject + how the author feels about the subject = the main point

Directions: Find the main point of "Vesuvius."

+

....
subject

=

....
how the author feels

....
main point

Understanding How
Essays Are Organized

Understanding how the essay is organized can make it easier for you to locate important information. As you know, a narrative essay usually follows a chronological (time) order.

• **Track the events in a narrative essay by looking at what happened first, second, third, and fourth.**

Directions: Record the events Pliny describes in "Vesuvius."

introduction → first event → second event → third event → fourth event → ending

introduction   Pliny and his mother decide to flee.

first event

second event

third event

fourth event

ending

Connect

The personal connections you make to the subject can help you meet your reading purpose.

- **Connect to an essay by recording your thoughts and feelings about the subject.**

Directions: Imagine yourself in Pliny the Younger's shoes. How would you have felt during the eruption?

I would have felt ....

....

....

After Reading

When you finish reading, take a moment or two to think about what you did and did not understand about the essay.

 Pause and Reflect

Ask yourself questions about the selection and your purpose for reading.

- **After you finish an essay, ask yourself, "How well did I meet my purpose?"**

Directions: Answer these questions about "Vesuvius."

Questions

What is the subject of the essay? ....

....

What does the author say about the subject? ....

....

How do you feel about the author's message? ....

....

Do you feel you've met your reading purpose? ....

....

Reread

Use the strategy of questioning the author if you're not 100 percent certain you understood what you read. Zero in on the part you're unsure of. Then ask a few questions. Imagine the author is sitting right there next to you.

• A powerful rereading strategy to use is questioning the author.

Directions: Write three questions for Pliny the Younger. Then write the answers you think he might have given.

Questioning the Author

Question #1: ....
....
....

Pliny's answer: ....
....
....

Question #2: ....
....
....

Pliny's answer: ....
....
....

Question #3: ....
....
....

Pliny's answer: ....
....

Remember

Good readers remember what they've read. Writing a summary can help.

• **A summary can help you remember the most important parts of an essay.**

Directions: Write a summary of "Vesuvius." Put into your own words what Pliny the Younger said. Then explain how the writing made you feel.

Summary

"Vesuvius"

Nonfiction

Reading a Biography

A biography is the story of a person's life. Most biographers write with two goals in mind: (1) They want to tell an interesting story about the events in the person's life. (2) They want to create a "portrait," or impression, of that person so that readers can understand what he or she was really like.

Before Reading

Practice using the reading process and the strategy of looking for cause and effect with this excerpt from a biography of Abraham Lincoln.

 A **Set a Purpose**

When reading a biography, your purpose is to find out as much as you can about the subject's life so that you can form an impression of him or her.

• To set your purpose, ask a question about the biographical subject.

Directions: Write your purpose for reading the biography of Lincoln. Then tell what you already know about his childhood.

My purpose:

....

....

....

Here's what I already know about Lincoln's childhood:

....

....

....

....

Preview

As always, your first step is to preview the text. Pay particular attention to the biography's front and back covers and any introductory pages.

Directions: Preview *The Boys' Life of Abraham Lincoln*. Make notes below.

◄ Preview Chart

Who is the subject of the biography?

What is the main time period of the biography?

How do you know?

What did you learn from the table of contents?

What did you notice about the introductory art?

Back Cover

Front Cover

Abraham Lincoln was the 16th president of the United States, and one of the great leaders of the free world. His rise from humble beginnings to worldwide acclaim is one of America's most famous success stories.

Helen Nicolay's biography The Boy's Life of Abraham Lincoln *was first published in 1906. Since then, millions of readers have enjoyed this classic work.*

A Biography

The Boys' Life of Abraham Lincoln
by HELEN NICOLAY

Table of Contents

C Plan

Next make a plan. Choose a strategy that can help you understand the facts of the subject's life and how they affected his or her personality.

• **Use the strategy of looking for cause and effect to help you get more from a biography.**

During Reading

Now do a careful reading of the excerpt. Take notes about key events as you go.

D Read with a Purpose

Keep your reading purpose in mind. Remember that you are trying to form an impression of the subject of the biography.

Directions: Read the passage from Lincoln's biography. Make notes in the "Causes/Events" side of this Cause-Effect Organizer as you read. You'll return to the "Effect" box later.

Cause-Effect Organizer

Causes/Events

Effect

The Lincoln family moved from Rock Spring Farm to Knob Creek, Kentucky.

Lincoln was

Write the events the author describes here.

and

from *The Boys' Life of Abraham Lincoln* by Helen Nicolay

from Chapter 1 A President's Childhood

Then they [Abraham Lincoln's parents and older sister] moved to a small farm thirteen miles from Elizabethtown, which they bought on credit, the country being yet so new that there were places to be had for mere promises to pay. Farms obtained on such terms were usually of very poor quality, and this one of Thomas Lincoln's was no exception to the rule. A cabin ready to be occupied stood on it, however; and not far away, hidden in a pretty clump of trees and bushes, was a fine spring of water, because of which the place was known as Rock Spring Farm. In the cabin on this farm the future President of the United States was born on February 12, 1809, and here the first four years of his life were spent. Then the Lincolns moved to a much bigger and better farm on Knob Creek, six miles from Hodgenville, which Thomas Lincoln bought, again on credit, selling the larger part of it soon afterward to another purchaser. Here they remained until Abraham was seven years old.

About this early part of his childhood almost nothing is known. He never talked of these days, even to his most intimate friends. To the pioneer child a farm offered much that a town lot could not give him—space; woods to roam in; Knob Creek with its running water and its deep, quiet pools for a playfellow; berries to be hunted for in summer and nuts in autumn; while all the year round birds and small animals pattered across his path to people the solitude in place of human companions. The boy had few comrades. He wandered about playing his lonesome little games, and when these were finished returned to the small and cheerless cabin. Once, when asked what he remembered about the War of 1812 with Great Britain, he replied: "Only this: I had been fishing one day and had caught a little fish, which I was taking home. I met a soldier in the road, and having always been told at home that we must be good to soldiers, I gave him my fish." It is only a glimpse into his life, but it shows the solitary, generous child and the patriotic household.

Stop and Organize
What important events have you read about so far? Make notes on your Cause-Effect Organizer (page 71).

It was while living on this farm that Abraham and his sister Sarah first began going to A-B-C schools. Their earliest teacher was Zachariah Riney, who taught near the Lincoln cabin; the next was Caleb Hazel, four miles away. . . .

Though only seven years old, Abraham was unusually large and strong for his age, and he helped his father in all this heavy labor of clearing the farm. In after years, Mr. Lincoln said that an ax "was put into his hands at once, and from that till within

from *The Boys' Life of Abraham Lincoln* by Helen Nicolay, continued

his twenty-third year he was almost constantly handling that most useful instrument—less, of course, in ploughing and harvesting seasons." At first the Lincolns and their seven or eight neighbors lived in the unbroken forest. They had only the tools and household goods they brought with them, or such things as they could fashion with their own hands. There was no sawmill to saw lumber. The village of Gentryville was not even begun. Breadstuff could be had only by sending young Abraham seven miles on horseback with a bag of corn to be ground in a hand grist-mill.

About the time the new cabin was ready relatives and friends followed from Kentucky, and some of these in turn occupied the half-faced camp. During the autumn a severe and mysterious sickness broke out in their little settlement, and a number of people died, among them the mother of young Abraham. There was no help to be had beyond what the neighbors could give each other. The nearest doctor lived fully thirty miles away. There was not even a minister to conduct the funerals. Thomas Lincoln made the coffins for the dead out of green lumber cut from the forest trees with a whipsaw, and they were laid to rest in a clearing in the woods. Months afterward, largely through the efforts of the sorrowing boy, a preacher who chanced to come that way was induced to hold a service and preach a sermon over the grave of Mrs. Lincoln.

Stop and Organize

What important events have you read about so far?
Make notes on your Cause-Effect Organizer (page 71).

Her death was indeed a serious blow to her husband and children. Abraham's sister, Sarah, was only eleven years old, and the tasks and cares of the little household were altogether too heavy for her years and experience. Nevertheless they struggled bravely through the winter and following summer; then in the autumn of 1819 Thomas Lincoln went back to Kentucky and married Sarah Bush Johnston, whom he had known, and it is said courted, when she was only Sally Bush. She had married about the time Lincoln married Nancy Hanks, and her husband had died, leaving her with three children. She came of a better station in life than Thomas, and was a woman with an excellent mind as well as a warm and generous heart. The household goods that she brought with her to the Lincoln home filled a four-horse wagon, and not only were her own children well clothed and cared for, but she was able at once to provide little Abraham and Sarah with comforts to which they had been strangers during the whole of their young lives. Under her wise management all jealousy was avoided between the two sets of children; urged on by her stirring example, Thomas Lincoln supplied the

from *The Boys' Life of Abraham Lincoln* by Helen Nicolay, continued

yet unfinished cabin with floor, door, and windows, and life became more comfortable for all its inmates, contentment if not happiness reigning in the little home.

The new stepmother quickly became very fond of Abraham, and encouraged him in every way in her power to study and improve himself. The chances for this were few enough. Mr. Lincoln has left us a vivid picture of the situation. "It was," he once wrote, "a wild region, with many bears and other wild animals still in the woods. There I grew up. There were some schools, so-called, but no qualification was ever required of a teacher beyond "readin', writin', and cipherin' to the Rule of Three. If a straggler supposed to understand Latin happened to sojourn in the neighborhood, he was looked upon as a wizard."

The schoolhouse was a low cabin of round logs, with split logs or "puncheons" for a floor, split logs roughly leveled with an ax and set up on legs for benches, and holes cut out in the logs and the space filled in with squares of greased paper for window-panes. The main light came in through the open door. Very often Webster's "Elementary Spelling-book" was the only textbook. This was the kind of school most common in the middle West during Mr. Lincoln's boyhood, though already in some places there were schools of a more pretentious character. Indeed, back in Kentucky, at the very time that Abraham, a child of six, was learning his letters from Zachariah Riney, a boy only a year older was attending a Catholic seminary in the very next county. It is doubtful if they ever met, but the destinies of the two were strangely interwoven, for the older boy was Jefferson Davis, who became head of the Confederate government shortly after Lincoln was elected President of the United States.

Stop and Organize

What important events have you read about?
Make notes on your Cause-Effect Organizer (page 71).

Using the Strategy

As you read, think carefully about the "portrait" the writer has created. What is your impression of the subject of the biography?

Directions: Return to the "Effect" side of the Cause-Effect Organizer on page 71. Write three adjectives (descriptive words) for Lincoln. Refer to your preview and During Reading notes as needed.

Understanding How Biographies Are Organized

Good biographies explore key events in a subject's life. Your job as reader is to figure out how these events affected the subject. A Character Map can help.

Directions: Consider what you know about Abraham Lincoln. Make notes on this Character Map.

Character Map

What he said and did	How he looked and felt

Abraham Lincoln

What others thought about him	How I feel about him

Nonfiction

E Connect

Whenever you read a biography, think about your impression of the subject.

• **Record your own thoughts and feelings about the subject as you read.**

Directions: Tell how you felt as you were reading about Lincoln's childhood.

As I was reading the story of Lincoln's childhood, I felt

After Reading

When you finish a biography, think about what you've learned.
Have you found some events that shaped Lincoln's life?

F Pause and Reflect

Return to your reading purpose and decide whether you've accomplished
what you set out to do.

- **To reflect on your purpose, ask yourself, "Can I speak knowledgeably about the biographical subject?"**

<u>Directions:</u> Complete this chart. If you have trouble, do some rereading.

Events in Lincoln's Life	
Three important events in Lincoln's life	**How these events may have affected his feelings about himself or others**
1.	
2.	
3.	

G Reread

If you haven't formed a strong impression of the subject, you may need
to do some rereading.

- **The strategy of outlining can help you organize information you find on your rereading.**

NAME _____

Directions: Take a second look at the reading. Then make notes on this Outline.

Outline

Abraham Lincoln

  I. Early Years

      A. Important event: The Lincoln family moves to Kentucky.

      B. Important event:

  II. School-age Years

      A. Important event:

      B. Important event:

      C. Important event:

H **Remember**

Do your best to remember what you've learned about the biographical subject.

• **Use Study Cards to help you retain what you've learned.**

Directions: Complete this Study Card about Abraham Lincoln's childhood. Write important details from the reading.

Study Card

Abraham Lincoln's Childhood

Reading an Autobiography

An autobiography is the story of the writer's own life. Most autobiographers write with two purposes in mind. (1) They want to tell the story of their lives in an interesting and dramatic way (2) They want to create a flattering self-portrait readers can relate to and admire.

Before Reading

Your job when reading an autobiography is to learn about the writer's life and then decide how you feel about him or her. Use the reading process and the strategy of synthesizing to help. Practice here with a selection from social reformer Jane Addams's autobiography.

 A **Set a Purpose**

Ask yourself these two questions as you read: "What kind of life did the autobiographer have?" and "How do I feel about him or her?"

• To set your purpose, ask two questions about the autobiographer.

Directions: Write two questions about Jane Addams and *Twenty Years at Hull House*. Finding answers to these questions will be your purpose for reading.

My Purpose

Question #1: What kind of Life did this person have

Question #2: How do I feel about him or her

NAME _____

B Preview

Keep your purpose questions in mind as you preview the autobiography.

Directions: Preview the front and back covers of *Twenty Years at Hull House*. Complete the sticky notes.

Back Cover

Learn about the life and times of Jane Addams, American social reformer and Nobel laureate.

In 1889, Jane Addams established Hull House in Chicago, one of the first settlement houses in the United States. As spokesperson for the downtrodden, Addams became involved in social reform at the national level and was a pioneer in the movement for women's rights. Addams's groundbreaking autobiography, *Twenty Years at Hull House,* was published to critical acclaim in 1910. Her objective for writing this book was to "open the eyes of the public" to the desolation and despair that marked the lives of so many Americans of the time.

Front Cover

Great Men and Women in American History Series

Twenty Years at Hull House

by **Jane Addams**

Nonfiction

Key events I noticed:

Event #1 Jane Addams
established Hull House

Event #2 Addams became
involved in social reform

Event #3

Title Twenty Years
at Hull House

Author Jane Addams

C Plan

When you've finished previewing, make a reading plan that can help you meet your purpose.

• **Use the strategy of synthesizing to help you see the "full picture" that the autobiographer presents.**

Synthesizing is like gathering up the pieces of a puzzle and figuring out how they fit together.

During Reading

Now do a careful reading of the following excerpt from Addams's book. Make notes as you go.

Directions: Write notes about Addams on this Character Trait Web. Use details from the reading to support your ideas. Add traits as you read. Each time you find a new trait, supply at least two pieces of proof from the text.

Character Trait Web

Proof: Worked in Candy factory

Proof: Women Sewing

Trait: Hard-working

Jane Addams

Trait: Loved Children

Proof:

Proof:

D Read with a Purpose

Keep your purpose in mind as you read and make notes. Remember that you're looking for information about Addams's life. You also want to form an *impression* of her.

from *Twenty Years at Hull House* by Jane Addams

Chapter X
Pioneer Labor Legislation in Illinois

Our very first Christmas at Hull House, when we as yet knew nothing of child labor, a number of little girls refused the candy which was offered them as part of the Christmas good cheer, saying simply that they "worked in a candy factory and could not bear the sight of it." We discovered that for six weeks they had worked from seven in the morning until nine at night, and they were exhausted as well as satiated. The sharp consciousness of stern economic conditions was thus thrust upon us in the midst of the season of good will. During the same winter three boys from a Hull House club were injured at one machine in a neighboring factory for lack of a guard which would have cost but a few dollars. When the injury of one of these boys resulted in his death, we felt quite sure that the owners of the factory would share our horror and remorse, and that they would do everything possible to prevent the recurrence of such a tragedy. To our surprise they did nothing whatever, and I made my first acquaintance then with those pathetic documents signed by the parents of working children, that they will make no claim for damages resulting from "carelessness."

The visits we made in the neighborhood constantly discovered women sewing upon sweatshop work, and often they were assisted by incredibly small children. I remember a little girl of four who pulled out basting threads hour after hour, sitting on a stool at the feet of her Bohemian mother, a little bunch of human misery. But even for that there was no legal redress, for the only child-labor law in Illinois, with any provision for enforcement, had been secured by the coal miners' unions, and was confined to children employed in mines. We learned to know many families in which the working children contributed to the support of their parents, not only because they spoke English better than the older immigrants and were willing to take lower wages, but because their parents gradually found it easy to live upon their earnings.

Stop and Record

Make notes on your Character Trait Web (page 80).
What inferences can you make about Jane Addams?

Nonfiction

from *Twenty Years at Hull House* by Jane Addams, **continued**

A South Italian peasant who has picked olives and packed oranges from his toddling babyhood cannot see at once the difference between the outdoor healthy work which he had performed in the varying seasons and the long hours of monotonous factory life which his child encounters when he goes to work in Chicago. An Italian father came to us in great grief over the death of his eldest child, a little girl of twelve, who had brought the largest wages into the family fund. In the midst of his genuine sorrow he said: "She was the oldest kid I had. Now I shall have to go back to work again until the next one is able to take care of me." The man was only thirty-three and had hoped to retire from work at least during the winters. No foreman cared to have him in a factory, untrained and unintelligent as he was. It was much easier for his bright, English-speaking little girl to get a chance to paste labels on a box than for him to secure an opportunity to carry pig iron. The effect on the child was what no one concerned thought about, in the abnormal effort she made thus prematurely to bear the weight of life. . . .

While we found many pathetic cases of child labor and hard-driven victims of the sweating system who could not possibly earn enough in the short busy season to support themselves during the rest of the year, it became evident that we must add carefully collected information to our general impression of neighborhood conditions if we would make it of any genuine value.

Stop and Record
Make notes on your Character Trait Web (page 80). What was Addams's personality like?

There was at that time no statistical information on Chicago industrial conditions, and Mrs. Florence Kelley, an early resident of Hull House, suggested to the Illinois State Bureau of Labor that they investigate the sweating system in Chicago with its attendant child labor. The head of the Bureau adopted this suggestion and engaged Mrs. Kelley to make the investigation. When the report was presented to the Illinois Legislature, a special committee was appointed to look into the Chicago conditions. I well recall that on the Sunday the members of this commission came to dine at Hull House, our hopes ran high, and we believed that at last some of the worst ills under which our neighbors were suffering would be brought to an end.

As a result of its investigations, this committee recommended to the Legislature the provisions which afterward became those of the first factory law of Illinois, regulating the sanitary conditions of the sweatshop and fixing fourteen as the age at which a child might be employed.

Using the Strategy

When you synthesize, you examine key topics or ideas in a reading and then see how they all work together.

• **Use Key Topic Notes to help you zero in on one or more parts of the autobiographer's life.**

Directions: Make some Key Topic Notes about Jane Addams. Read the key topics in the left column. Write your notes in the right column.

Key Topic Notes

Key Topics	Notes from Reading
work	
hopes and dreams	
worries	
beliefs	

Nonfiction

Understanding How
Autobiographies Are Organized

Most autobiographers tell their life stories in chronological (time) order. You can use a Timeline to track the events the writer describes. Begin with significant dates or years. If dates aren't given, note important events, or milestones, in the writer's life.

Directions: Complete this Timeline. Write one event in each box.

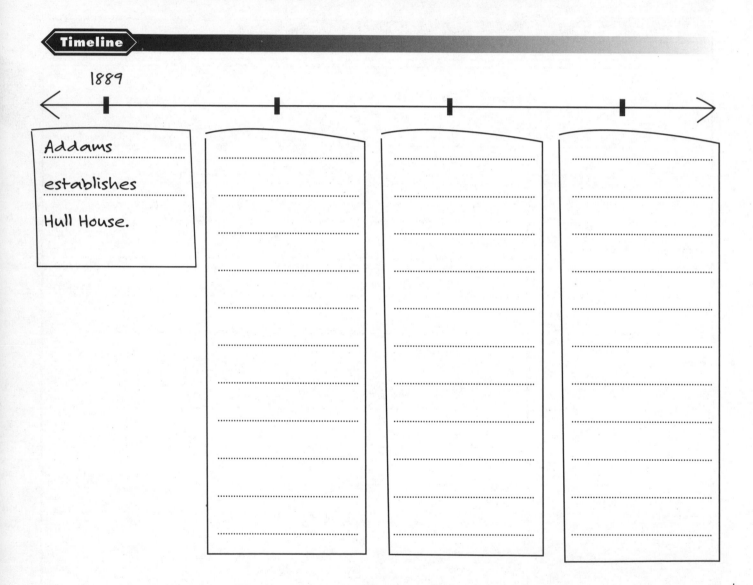

Timeline

1889

Addams
establishes
Hull House.

Another feature common to autobiographies is that they are written in the first person. Look for pronouns such as *I, we,* and *our.*

Directions: Go back to the selection from *Twenty Years at Hull House.* Find at least three examples that show this book was written in the first person. Highlight or underline the sentences in which the examples appear.

Connect

Remember that a part of your purpose is to decide how you feel about the autobiographer. When you examine your feelings, you make a connection to the text.

• **Ask yourself, "How do I feel about the autobiographer?"**

Directions: Complete this chart. Use your notes from the reading.

Inference Chart

What Jane Addams said or did	My impression of her
She opened Hull House to help the poor.	She was a caring person. She cared about people who didn't have enough.
"We discovered that for six weeks they had worked from seven in the morning until nine at night, and they were exhausted as well as satiated."	
". . . I made my first acquaintance then with those pathetic documents signed by the parents of working children, that they will make no claim for damages resulting from 'carelessness.'"	
She worried about the child labor problem.	
She recommended that the state Bureau of Labor investigate the sweating system in Chicago.	

Nonfiction

After Reading

When you finish reading, take a moment to think about what you've learned.

 Pause and Reflect

Reflect on the self-portrait the writer has created.

• **Ask yourself, "What is my impression of the autobiographer?"**

<u>Directions:</u> Answer these questions about Jane Addams. Refer to your notes as needed.

Who was Jane Addams? ....

....

....

What was she like? ....

....

....

What did she do that was important? ....

....

....

....

Circle *would* or *would not.*

I would / would not like to find out more about Addams because ....

....

....

....

NAME ....

FOR USE WITH PAGES 204–217

 Reread

If you're having trouble forming a clear impression of the autobiographer, you may need to do some rereading. As you reread, watch for the events that shaped the autobiographer's personality.

• **Use a Cause-Effect Organizer to track life-shaping events.**

Directions: Read the description of Jane Addams on the right side of the organizer. Then list events from her life that may have had an effect on her personality.

Cause-Effect Organizer

Causes

She listened to parents tell of the hardships their children were suffering.

....
....

Effect

Addams was a social reformer who fought on behalf of women, children, and immigrants.

....
....

 Remember

It's important to remember your general impression of the autobiographer so that you can speak knowledgeably about him or her.

• **Writing your opinion of the autobiographer can help you retain what you've learned.**

Directions: Write your opinion of Jane Addams here. Then explain.

Here's how I feel about Addams after reading her words from her autobiography:

....
....

Reading a Newspaper Article

You can learn what's happening around the world and in your community by reading a newspaper. Take what you learn here and use it the next time you read a newspaper article for a school assignment.

Before Reading

Use the reading process and the strategy of reading critically to help you read and understand a newspaper article about the San Francisco earthquake.

A Set a Purpose

Your main purpose when reading a newspaper article is to find out what it's about.

• **To set your purpose, take several words from the headline and use them in a question.**

Directions: Write your purpose for reading "Earthquake and Fire: San Francisco in Ruins" below. Then write some prereading questions about the article.

My purpose:

....

....

....

My prereading questions:

....

....

....

....

....

B **Preview**

The lead, or first few paragraphs, of a newspaper article tells *who, what, where, when*, and *why*.

Directions: Read the headnote and first paragraph of the earthquake article, which appears on page 91. Then complete as much of this 5 W's Organizer as you can.

5 W's Organizer

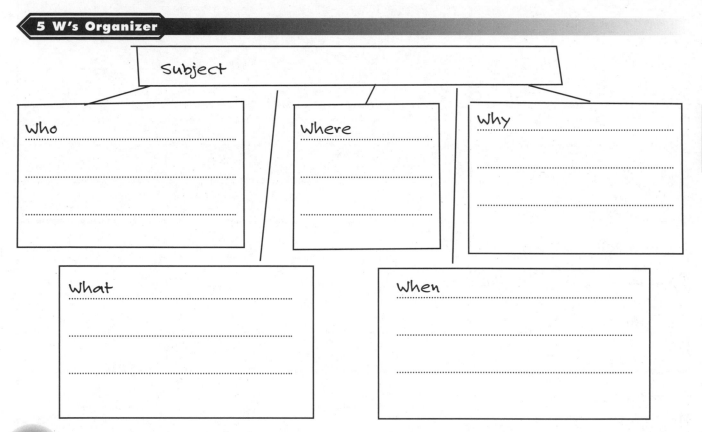

Subject

Who

Where

Why

What

When

C **Plan**

Next make a plan. Choose a reading strategy that can help you understand and evaluate the article you're about to read.

• **Use the strategy of reading critically with newspaper articles.**

During Reading

Now you're ready to do a careful reading of the article.

Directions: Read "Earthquake and Fire: San Francisco in Ruins." Use the Critical Reading Chart on the next page for your During Reading notes.

Nonfiction

Critical Reading Chart

Questions	My Thoughts
What are facts and what are opinions?	
Who is telling the story? Are the reporter's facts well supported by evidence?	
Are the sources authoritative and reliable?	
What's the other side of the story?	

D Read with a Purpose

Keep your purpose in mind as you read. Use your Critical Reading Chart
to help you separate facts from opinions.

90

What follows is the front page article from the combined Call-Chronicle-Examiner *that was published and distributed in San Francisco on April 19. Although the* Call, Chronicle, *and* Examiner *were normally fierce competitors, the earthquake and ensuing fires damaged the offices and presses of these three newspapers and forced them to join together to publish a joint Earthquake edition.*

The article about the earthquake that appeared that day was read by millions of people around the country. Two of the facts presented in the article were actually incorrect. Martial law was never declared in San Francisco, although some officials felt it might be necessary. The second fact, that the earthquake lasted 48 seconds, is also in error. This devastating quake, which registered 8.3 on the Richter scale, lasted a full minute or longer in all areas of San Francisco.

The Call — Chronicle — Examiner

Thursday, April 19, 1906

EARTHQUAKE AND FIRE: SAN FRANCISCO IN RUINS

Fire Rages after Trembler

Death and destruction have been the fate of San Francisco. Shaken by a trembler at 5:13 o'clock yesterday morning, the shock lasting 48 seconds, and scourged by flames, that raged diametrically in all directions, the city is a mass of smoldering ruins. At six o'clock last evening the flames, seemingly playing with increased vigor, threatened to destroy such sections as their fury had spared during the earlier portion of the day. Building their path in a triangular circuit from the start in the early morning, they jockeyed as the day waned, left the business section, which they had entirely devastated, and skipped in a dozen directions to the residence portions. As night fell they had made their way over into the North Beach section and springing anew to the south they reached out along the shipping section down the bay shore, over the hills and across toward Third and Townsend streets.

Stop and Record

What facts about the earthquake does the reporter present? Record them on your Critical Reading Chart (page 90).

"Earthquake and Fire: San Francisco in Ruins," continued

Thousands Left Homeless

Warehouses, wholesale houses and manufacturing concerns fell in their path. This completed the destruction of the entire district known as the "South of Market Street." How far they are reaching to the south across the channel cannot be told as this part of the city is shut off from San Francisco papers. After darkness, thousands of the homeless were making their way with their blankets and scant provisions to Golden Gate Park and the beach to find shelter. Those in the homes on the hills just north of the Hayes Valley wrecked section piled their belongings in the streets and express wagons and automobiles were hauling the things away to the sparsely settled sections. Everybody in San Francisco is prepared to leave the city, for the belief is firm that San Francisco will be totally destroyed.

Businesses Entirely Destroyed

Downtown everything is in ruins. Not a business house stands. Theaters are crumbled into heaps. Factories and commission houses lie smoldering on their former sites.

All of the newspaper plants have been rendered useless, the *Call* and the *Examiner* buildings, excluding the *Call*'s editorial rooms on Stevenson Street, being entirely destroyed.

It is estimated that the loss in San Francisco will reach from $150,000,000 to $200,000,000. These figures are in the rough and nothing can be told until partial accounting is taken.

On every side there was death and suffering yesterday. Hundreds were injured, either burned, crushed or struck by falling pieces from the buildings, and one died while on the operating table at Mechanics' Pavilion, improvised as a hospital for the comfort and care of 300 of the injured.

Stop and Record

What opinions about the earthquake does the reporter present? Record them on your Critical Reading Chart (page 90).

At Least 500 Dead; Rescuers Work Like Fiends

The number of dead is not known but it is estimated that at least 500 met their death in the horror.

At nine o'clock, under a special message from President Roosevelt, the city was placed under martial law. Hundreds of troops patrolled the streets and drove the crowds back, while hundreds more were set at work assisting the fire and police departments. The strictest orders were issued, and in true military spirit the soldiers obeyed. During the afternoon three thieves met their death by rifle bullets while at work in the ruins. The curious were driven back at the breasts of the horses that the cavalrymen rode and all the crowds were forced from the level district to the hilly section beyond to the north.

The water supply was entirely cut off, and maybe it was just as well, for the lines of fire department would have been

"Earthquake and Fire: San Francisco in Ruins," continued

absolutely useless at any stage. Assistant Chief Dougherty supervised the work of his men and early in the morning it was seen that the only possible chance to save the city lay in efforts to check the flames by use of dynamite. During the day a blast could be heard in any section at intervals of only a few minutes, and buildings not destroyed by fire were blown to atoms. But

through the gaps made the flames jumped and although the failures of the heroic efforts of the police, firemen and soldiers were at times sickening, the work was continued with a desperation that will live as one of the features of the terrible disaster. Men worked like fiends to combat the laughing, roaring, onrushing fire demon.

Stop and Record

How does the reporter feel about the disaster?
Make notes on your Critical Reading Chart (page 90).

Using the Strategy

Reading critically means reading slowly and carefully. Consider the evidence the writer provides. Is it reliable?

• Use your Critical Reading Chart to evaluate the evidence.

Directions: Use the notes in your Critical Reading Chart on page 90 to answer these questions.

Evaluate the Evidence

What evidence is presented?

How convincing is the evidence?

Understanding How
Newspaper Articles Are Organized

Most newspaper articles follow a standard organization called an *inverted pyramid*. See page 229 of your handbook for details.

Directions: Go back to your 5 W's Organizer on page 89. Review the details from the lead. Then show the organization of the earthquake article on this inverted pyramid.

Inverted Pyramid

Most important details:

Detail #1 ....

....

Detail #2 ....

....

Detail #3 ....

....

Less important details:

Detail #4 ....

....

Detail #5 ....

....

Least important details:

Detail #6 ....

....

....

Detail #7 ....

....

E **Connect**

You can make a connection to the reading by figuring out how the article applies to your own life or how it makes you feel.

> • **Making a personal connection to a newspaper article can help you feel more involved in what you're reading.**

The article about the San Francisco earthquake made me feel

....

because

....

....

....

....

....

After Reading

After you finish an article, think about what you learned.

 F **Pause and Reflect**

At this point, consider whether you've met your reading purpose.

> • **Ask yourself some questions about the article you just finished.**

Directions: Complete this reading checklist.

Reading Checklist

Checklist	Yes	No
I can answer who, what, where, when, and why questions.		
I know which details are facts and which are opinions in the article.		
I understand the main idea of the article.		
I can find three or more details the reporter uses as support for the main idea.		

Reread

If you feel you haven't fully learned the facts of the article, you'll need to do some rereading.

• **Use the strategy of summarizing when you reread.**

Directions: Make Summary Notes about the earthquake article.

Summary Notes

Article Headline: ....

Subject: ....

Main Idea: ....

Detail #1: ....

Detail #2: ....

Detail #3: ....

Detail #4: ....

Detail #5: ....

....

H Remember

If you can remember the most important details of an article, you can speak knowledgeably about the subject later.

• **Writing a brief summary can help you remember an article.**

Directions: Write a brief summary of "Earthquake and Fire: San Francisco in Ruins." Include only the most important details.

Summary

....

....

....

....

Reading a Magazine Article

If your assignment is to read and respond to a magazine article, which tools and strategies should you use, and how should you use them? Practice here.

Before Reading

Use the reading process and the strategy of questioning the author to help you read and respond to an article about bald eagles.

A Set a Purpose

Before reading, set your purpose. Ask yourself, "What do I hope to learn from the article?"

• **Use keywords from the title of the article to form a reading purpose question.**

<u>Directions:</u> Write your purpose for reading a magazine article called "Sweet Victory: The Return of the Bald Eagle." Then predict what you think the article is about.

My purpose: ....

....

....

....

My predictions: ....

....

....

....

....

....

Nonfiction

Preview

When you preview, look for clues about the **subject** of the article. Take a careful look at the title, any photographs or illustrations, headings or large type, and the first paragraph.

Directions: Preview the magazine article that follows. Write your preview notes here.

Preview Notes

The title of the article:

What I noticed about the art:

What I learned from the headings:

What I learned from the first paragraph:

What I learned from the last paragraph:

Here's what I know about the topic:

Bald Eagle: Facts to Know

Common name: bald eagle

Class: Aves

Order: Falconiformes

Life Span: up to 30 years in the wild; longer in captivity

Habitat: Most live and nest near coastlines, rivers, lakes, wet prairies, and coastal pine lands in North America from Canada south into Florida and Baja, California. Many bald eagles return to the same nests again and again. Each year they add a few more twigs and branches and call it home for another season.

Habits: Bald eagles can swim. They use an overhead wing movement that is very much like the butterfly stroke. When they're not swimming, they're soaring through the air at speeds of 20 to 40 m.p.h. When they dive, they do so at speeds of over 100 m.p.h.

Diet: Bald eagles hunt fish that swim close to the surface, small mammals, waterfowl, and dead animal matter.

Appearance: The bald eagle is not really bald. In fact, its head is covered with white feathers. People began calling this type of eagle a "bald eagle," since the Old English word *balde* means "white."

Sweet Victory The Return of the Bald Eagle

"Sweet Victory: The Return of the Bald Eagle," continued

The bald eagle is back. You can see them sometimes, swooping and diving in Florida and Montana. You can spot their distinctive shadows in the deserts of Arizona and their claw prints in the deep snow of Alaska. In fact, there are so many bald eagles now that the United States Fish and Wildlife Service has taken them off the endangered and threatened lists altogether. But is this a good idea?

Many people argue that with the eagle taken off these lists, the government and the public can then focus on a different endangered species—one that is closer to extinction. Others argue that the bald eagle, because of its status as our national bird, should remain on the protected lists forever. In any event, the issue pits the government against the general public, and the general public against those who hunt and fish to make their living. So who is in the best position to answer this question? Should it be them or us or you? Before you decide, you need to learn the bald eagle's long and difficult history.

Stop and Question

What is the subject of the article and why did the author want to write about it? (Write your answer on page 103.)

What You Should Know about the Bald Eagle

The bald eagle is our national bird. It is the only eagle unique to North America. This means that you won't find a bald eagle if you travel to South America, for example, or Asia, or anywhere else in the world. This is one of the things that makes the bald eagle special.

Today, the bald eagle—whose scientific name is *Haliaeetus leucocephalus*—is found all over North America, from Alaska and Canada to northern Mexico. Close to 60 percent of them, however, make their homes in Alaska, where the salmon is plentiful.

Most bald eagles are around three feet tall, with a wing span of seven feet. They have a life span of approximately 30 years in the wild, and close to 40 years in captivity. Most male bald eagles weigh around 9 pounds. Females tend to weigh 13 pounds or more.

For centuries, poets, storytellers, and artists have celebrated the freedom and beauty of this bird of prey. The bald eagle is the subject of many famous works, including this poem by Alfred, Lord Tennyson:

The Eagle
He clasps the crag with crooked
  hands;
Close to the sun in lonely lands,
Ring'd with the azure world,
  he stands.

The wrinkled sea beneath him
  crawls;
He watches from his mountain walls,
And like a thunderbolt he falls.

The Decline of the Bald Eagle

At one time, around a half million bald eagles lived in North America. Before the first European settlers arrived, they inhabited every large river and lake in America and Canada. They nested in

"Sweet Victory: The Return of the Bald Eagle," continued

forty-five of the lower forty-eight states. They tended to congregate on the Hudson River, and were extremely abundant along the coast of Maine. Although fishermen thought of them as pests, farmers welcomed bald eagles and their habit of eating rodents and other small animals.

As is the case with many species of animals, however, the bald eagle population began to decline as the human population grew. More and more humans meant more and more fishermen competing for the bald eagle's primary food source. Not surprisingly, the eagles lost this competition.

Humans also posed a threat to the bald eagles' natural habitat. Colonists who settled the West destroyed the natural habitat of the eagles, leaving them fewer places to nest and hunt. As a result, the population of bald eagles declined dramatically during the late 1800s.

The Public Sounds the Alarm

In the early 1930s, the public took notice that the bald eagle population was decreasing. Local and state groups began petitioning the government for help. Ten years later, in 1940, the Bald Eagle Act was passed. This act made it illegal to "take, transport, sell, barter, trade, import and export" the bald eagle. In addition, possession of a feather or other body part became a federal offense. Those who disobeyed the new law risked fines of up to $10,000 and/or imprisonment.

The Bald Eagle Act alone might have saved the species had it not been for the invention of pesticides. During the 1940s, farmers began spraying DDT and other pesticides on their crops in an attempt to control insects. Small animals ate the crops, and birds of prey ate the small animals.

Over the next ten years, thousands of bald eagles dropped dead from pesticide poisoning.

Even more alarming, environmental groups discovered that DDT harmed not only the adult birds, but also the eggs that had yet to be laid. Generations of eagle eggs thinned to the point that the shell could no longer withstand the incubation period. Countless eagle eggs cracked and the unborn eaglets were crushed. Those eggs that were not cracked often did not hatch due to high levels of DDT and other poisons.

Stop and Question
How does the author feel about the bald eagle? (Write your answer on page 103.)

Endangerment and Recovery

In the late 1960s and early 1970s, many states placed the bald eagle on their endangered species list. On July 4, 1976, the U.S. Fish and Wildlife Service stepped in and listed the bald eagle as a national endangered species. It was quite possible, environmentalists warned, that the bald eagle would soon be extinct.

For the next thirty years, federal and state agencies, along with private organizations, worked to save the bald eagle. DDT and other pesticides were banned, and gradually the poisons began leaving the eagles' systems. Countless eagle eggs were incubated and hatched by scientists working in eagle preserves. The eaglets born in the preserves were quickly released into the wild.

Little by little, the bald eagle population

"Sweet Victory: The Return of the Bald Eagle," continued

came back. By the late 1980s, there were close to 40,000 bald eagles in North America. More and more eagles were released into the wild, and people knew to leave them alone. Soon the species was flourishing.

The recovery has been so spectacular, in fact, that the bald eagle was downgraded to a "threatened" rather than an "endangered" species. In 1999, President Bill Clinton announced that the bald eagle was no longer in danger of extinction, and that the U.S. Fish and Wildlife Service proposed that it be declared fully recovered. This meant the bald eagle was taken off the endangered and threatened lists.

The Future

The bald eagle continues to be protected by the Bald Eagle Protection Act. This means that it is illegal to hunt bald eagles or interfere with their habitats. The worry is that federal and state agencies will no longer actively work to *increase* populations. Some environmentalists feel that if this happens, the bald eagle population will plateau, or level out, and then begin decreasing again.

Stop and Question
What is the author's message about the bald eagle?
(Write your answer on page 103).

Plan

After your preview, make your purpose more specific. What is an additional purpose-setting question you'd like to ask about the bald eagle article?

My purpose question: ....

....

Then choose a strategy that can help you understand the subject and main idea of the article.

- **Use the strategy of questioning the author to help you get *more* from a magazine article.**

NAME

During Reading

Now go back and do a careful reading of the article. As you read, ask questions of the author.

 Read with a Purpose

Keep in mind your purpose for reading. Remember that you're looking for information about the subject of the article.

Directions: Ask these questions as you read. Then write your own question for the author. Answer it the way you think the author would.

◀ Questions and Answers

1. What is the subject of the article, and why did the author want to write about it?

My answer:

2. How does the author feel about the bald eagle?

My answer:

3. What is the author's message about the bald eagle?

My answer:

4. My question for the author:

My answer:

Using the Strategy

One of the reasons you question an author is to find out the main idea of the article.

• **Use a Main Idea Organizer to keep track of important information.**

Directions: Complete this Main Idea Organizer. Use your notes from the article about protecting the bald eagle.

◀ Main Idea Organizer

Subject:		
Main Idea:		
Detail 1	Detail 2	Detail 3

Understanding How
Magazine Articles Are Organized

Some magazine articles tell a story. A Story String can help you keep track of the events in the story.

Directions: Retell the eagle article on this Story String.

Story String

Bald eagles live in peace all over North America.

NAME ....

 Connect

Jot down your personal reactions to a magazine article as you read. Make additional comments later, after you finish.

- **Recording your reactions to an article can help you process and remember what you've learned.**

<u>Directions:</u> Circle *interesting* or *not interesting* in the statement. Then write what you would like to learn more about.

I thought the article was interesting / not interesting because

....

....

....

Here's what I'd like to learn more about:

....

....

After Reading

After you finish reading, decide whether or not you agree with the author's main idea.

 Pause and Reflect

Begin by reflecting on your purpose.

- **To reflect on your purpose, ask yourself, "Have I accomplished what I set out to do?"**

<u>Directions:</u> Check *yes* or *no* for the items on this list.

Reading Checklist

Reading Checklist	Yes	No
I understand the topic of the article.		
I know the main idea of the article.		
I understand why this topic is important.		

Reread

At this point, think about the author's viewpoint. Decide whether or not you agree.

- **Use the strategy of reading critically to evaluate the viewpoint and evidence presented.**

Directions: Write proof from the article that supports the author's viewpoint.

Viewpoint and Evidence Organizer

Subject: The bald eagle

Author's Viewpoint:

Facts and Statistics:

Personal Experiences:

H Remember

Using the information you've read can help you remember it.

- **To remember a magazine article, tell a friend about it or write a journal entry.**

Directions: Write your thoughts and ideas about "Sweet Victory: The Return of the Bald Eagle" in a journal entry. Tell what the article was about and how it made you feel.

Journal Entry

Focus on Persuasive Writing

Persuasive writing makes an argument. Your job is to understand and evaluate the argument the writer presents. This three-step plan can help.

Step 1: Find the topic and viewpoint.

The **topic** is the subject of the writing. The **viewpoint** is the author's opinion about the subject.

Directions: Read this newspaper editorial. Make notes about the topic and viewpoint.

Dairy Farm Proposal a Terrible Mistake

There is a proposal before the Bethel Township planning board that the old dairy farm on Route 234 be torn down and replaced with a multi-family housing development. This farm, which was once owned by the Jacobsen family, became the property of Bethel Township when the last surviving member of the family passed away last year.

For six months now, the township board has been reviewing proposals for this piece of land. Hundreds of citizens have suggested various uses for the land, including turning the property into a public park or a community pool and recreation center, but the planning board has rejected each and every one of these proposals for various reasons.

Now the *Bethel County Times* has revealed that the Bethel Township planning board is seriously considering a proposal by DelMar Builders to turn the land into a multi-family housing development. DelMar has said that they will pay the township the princely sum of $1,000,000 for the 20-acre property. They have also promised to give the development a "park-like" setting.

The topic is ....

....

....

....

"Dairy Farm Proposal a Terrible Mistake," continued

Believe it or not, the planning board seems to be in favor of this proposal. But what the members of this board fail to recognize is that the citizens of Bethel Township don't want a development that looks like a park. They want a park that *is* a park, one in which children can play safely and families can spend time together.

Take a moment today to call, write, or email your Bethel Township planning board representative. Let him or her know that you will not stand for yet another development. Make it clear that taking one of the last few open spaces in our township and turning it into a development will prove to be a terrible mistake.

The viewpoint is

Step 2: Locate support for the viewpoint.

Next, look for details that support the viewpoint.

Directions: Reread the editorial. Underline details that support the writer's viewpoint. Then complete the organizer.

Main Idea Organizer

Topic:		
Main Idea:		
Detail 1	**Detail 2**	**Detail 3**

Step 3: Evaluate the argument.

After you finish reading, decide how you feel about the argument.

Directions: Complete this Argument Chart. Write the viewpoint and support for it. Then evaluate the argument.

Argument Chart

Viewpoint	Support	My Opinion
	Detail #1	
	Detail #2	
	Detail #3	

Nonfiction

Focus on Speeches

The reading process can help you understand and evaluate a speaker's message. Follow these steps.

Step 1: Find important details.

Highlight or underline important details on your first reading.

Directions: Take notes as you read this speech. Then complete the 5 W's Organizer.

from "Ain't I a Woman?" by Sojourner Truth

Isabella Van Wagner, who renamed herself Sojourner Truth, was born a slave in New York in 1797. She gained her freedom when she was thirty years old, but not before she saw most of her thirteen children sold. She made her memorable speech "Ain't I a Woman?" at the 1851 Women's Convention in Akron, Ohio.

Well, children, where there is so much racket there must be something out of kilter. I think that 'twixt the Negroes of the South and the women at the North, all talking about rights, the white men will be in a fix pretty soon. But what's all this here talking about?

That man over there says that women need to be helped into carriages, and lifted over ditches, and to have the best place everywhere. Nobody ever helps me into carriages, or over mud-puddles, or gives me any best place! And ain't I a woman? Look at me! Look at my arm! I have ploughed and planted, and gathered into barns, and no man could head me! And ain't I a woman? I could work as much and eat as much as a man—when I could get it—and bear the lash as well! And ain't I a woman? I have borne thirteen children, and seen most all sold off to slavery, and when I cried out with my mother's grief, none but Jesus heard me! And ain't I a woman? Then they talk about this thing in the head; what's this they call it? [A member of audience whispers, "intellect."] That's it, honey. What's that got to do with women's rights or Negroes' rights? If my cup won't hold but a pint, and yours holds a quart, wouldn't you be mean not to let me have my little half measure full? Then that little man in black there, he says women can't have as much rights as men, 'cause Christ wasn't a woman! Where did your Christ come from? Where did your Christ come from? From God and a woman! Man had nothing to do with Him.

NAME ....

from "Ain't I a Woman?" by Sojourner Truth continued

If the first woman God ever made was strong enough to turn the world upside down all alone, these women together ought to be able to turn it back, and get it right side up again! And now they is asking to do it, the men better let them.

Obliged to you for hearing me, and now old Sojourner ain't got nothing more to say.

5 W's Organizer

Who gave the speech?	**When** was it given?
What is the subject?	**Why** was it given?

Where was it given?

Step 2: Decide on the speaker's purpose.

Next, think about the speaker's purpose.

Directions: Write Sojourner Truth's purpose on the lines below.

I think Sojourner Truth's purpose was to ....

....

....

Step 3: Identify the viewpoint and support.

The speaker's opinion or main point is called his or her "viewpoint."
Find the viewpoint and evidence the speaker uses to support the viewpoint.
You can use this formula.

.... + ...

Topic of the speech   What Truth says about the topic

= ....

                                        Her viewpoint

Directions: Use a Main Idea Organizer to examine Sojourner Truth's
viewpoint. Write the main idea and three pieces of support she offers
for her viewpoint.

Main Idea Organizer

Main Idea:		
Detail 1	Detail 2	Detail 3

Step 4: React to the speaker's message.

Understanding your own reaction to a speech can help you better
understand the speaker's message.

Directions: Complete these sentences. Refer to your notes as needed.

Sojourner Truth's speech made me feel this way: ....

....

After reading the speech, I wanted to ....

....

Focus on Real-world Writing

Real-world, or informational, writing can help you stay informed. Follow these steps to get more from a piece of real-world writing.

Step 1: Identify your purpose.

First, figure out your purpose for reading.

Directions: Look at this graduation announcement. What is your reading purpose?

My purpose is _____

_____ .

IMPORTANT IMPORTANT IMPORTANT IMPORTANT IMPORTANT

8TH GRADE GRADUATION
FRIDAY, JUNE 10
7:30 P.M.

On Friday, June 10

Rolling Meadow Middle School

will hold graduation ceremonies

for all 8th grade students and their families.

ARRIVAL TIME: All graduating 8th graders must arrive at the school cafeteria by 6:30 P.M. There will be a brief rehearsal before the ceremony begins.

DRESS: Girls must wear a navy blue skirt or pants with a white shirt. Boys must wear navy blue pants and a white shirt. No T-shirts or halter tops.

WHAT TO BRING: Students who bring purses, cameras, yearbooks, and backpacks must leave them in the cafeteria during the ceremony. If you're worried it might be stolen, leave it at home!

TICKETS: Tickets for the graduation are available in the school office. Due to space restrictions, only four tickets will be issued to each 8th grade student. No exceptions!

Step 2: Search for what you need to know.

Pay attention to information that is important to you.

Directions: Highlight the most important points in the graduation flier.
Use the information to complete this Web.

Web

Who:

Where:

What

Graduation

Ceremony

When:

Why:

Step 3: Remember the information.

Decide how the information in the writing affects you personally. Then figure out a way to remember it.

Directions: Write information about the graduation ceremony on this calendar page. Include only the most important details.

F r i d a y ,   J u n e 🔟

Memo: ....

....

....

....

....

....

....

....

Reading a Short Story

Short stories can be funny, serious, suspenseful, or just plain amazing. The key to reading them is asking—and answering—the right kinds of questions. Practice here with a famous story by Edgar Allan Poe.

Before Reading

Let the reading process and the strategy of using graphic organizers help you read and respond to the short story "The Tell-Tale Heart."

 A   Set a Purpose

Setting your purpose first, before you begin reading, will help you get *more* from a short story.

• **To set your purpose, turn the title of the story into a question.**

Directions: Write your purpose for reading Poe's story. Then predict what you think the story will be about.

My purpose: ....

....

....

....

My predictions: ....

....

....

....

....

....

B **Preview**

Always preview before you begin reading. Take a careful look at any background material and the first several paragraphs of the story. Highlight words and phrases you think are important.

Directions: Preview "The Tell-Tale Heart." Make notes on this Preview Chart.

Preview Chart

Questions	My Notes
What is the title of the story?	
Who is the author?	
What did you learn from the background section?	
What ideas did the first two paragraphs give you about the story?	
What images (mental pictures) came to mind as you were previewing? Make a sketch here:	

Fiction

What you need to know . . .

THE SELECTION "The Tell-Tale Heart" is one of Edgar Allan Poe's most famous short stories. In this work, Poe explores the theme of guilt and shows how a guilty person's conscience can create a far worse punishment than any judge or jury in the land. The idea that the guilty always suffer is one that Poe returned to again and again in his writing.

THE AUTHOR Although Edgar Allan Poe lived just forty short years, he was an amazingly prolific writer and is recognized as the inventor of the modern detective story. Along with his mysteries, Poe wrote a large number of gothic tales that demonstrate his mastery of dark settings, macabre plot twists, and terrifyingly real characters. In addition, Poe is recognized as an important American poet and critic.

Poe was born January 19, 1809, in Boston. His parents were actors. When his mother died two years later, he was taken into the house of John Allan, a businessman in Richmond, Virginia, and given the family name. As a young man, Poe went back to his own last name, often using just A. for his middle name.

Before he began writing seriously, Poe showed a lack of purpose. He enrolled at the University of Virginia but left before his first year was up when John Allan refused to pay the debts he'd accumulated. Poe tried military life. He first served as an enlisted man and then briefly attended West Point Academy, but he was dismissed for neglect of duty. He settled in Baltimore, Maryland, where he lived with his aunt and her daughter, Virginia. A few years later, Poe married Virginia. During these years, he worked for various periodicals in New York and Philadelphia. After his young wife died, he grieved very much for the remainder of his life.

THE THEME Guilt

LITERARY FOCUS Plot

FURTHER READING "The Raven" and "The Pit and the Pendulum" by Poe

The Tell-Tale Heart
by *Edgar Allan Poe*

"The Tell-Tale Heart" by Edgar Allan Poe

True!—nervous—very, very dreadfully nervous I had been and am! But why *will* you say that I am mad? The disease had sharpened my senses—not destroyed—not dulled them. Above all was the sense of hearing acute. I heard all things in the heaven and in the earth. . . . How, then, am I mad? Hearken! and observe how healthily— how calmly I can tell you the whole story.

It is impossible to tell how first the idea entered my brain; but once conceived, it haunted me day and night. Object there was none. Passion there was none. I loved the old man. He had never wronged me. He had never given me insult. For his gold I had no desire. I think it was his eye! Yes, it was this! One of his eyes resembled that of a vulture—a pale blue eye, with a film over it. Whenever it fell upon me, my blood ran cold; and so by degrees—very gradually—I made up my mind to take the life of the old man, and thus rid myself of the eye forever.

Now this is the point. You fancy me mad. Madmen know nothing. But you should have seen *me.* You should have seen how wisely I proceeded—with what caution— with what foresight—with what dissimulation I went to work!

I was never kinder to the old man than during the whole week before I killed him. And every night, about midnight, I turned the latch of his door and opened it—oh, so gently! And then, when I had made an opening sufficient for my head, I put in a dark lantern, all closed, closed, so that no light shone out, and then I thrust in my head. Oh, you would have laughed to see how cunningly I thrust it in! I moved it slowly— very, very slowly, so that I might not disturb the old man's sleep. It took me an hour to place my whole head within the opening so far that I could see him as he lay upon his bed. Ha!—would a madman have been so wise as this? And then, when my head was well in the room, I undid the lantern cautiously—oh, so cautiously—cautiously (for the hinges creaked)—I undid it just so much that a single thin ray fell upon the vulture eye. And this I did for seven long nights—every night just at midnight—but I found the eye always closed; and so it was impossible to do the work; for it was not the old man who vexed me, but his Evil Eye. And every morning, when the day broke, I went boldly into the chamber, and spoke courageously to him, calling him by name in a hearty tone, and inquiring how he had passed the night. So, you see, he would have been a very profound old man, indeed, to suspect that every night, just at twelve, I looked in upon him while he slept.

Stop and Record
Make some notes in the "Beginning" section of the Story Organizer (page 123).

Fiction

"The Tell-Tale Heart" by Edgar Allan Poe, continued

Upon the eighth night I was more than usually cautious in opening the door. A watch's minute hand moves more quickly than did mine. Never before that night had I felt the extent of my own powers—of my sagacity. I could scarcely contain my feelings of triumph. To think that there I was, opening the door, little by little, and he not even to dream of my secret deeds or thoughts. I fairly chuckled at the idea; and perhaps he heard me; for he moved on the bed suddenly, as if startled. Now you may think that I drew back—but no. His room was as black as pitch with the thick darkness (for the shutters were tightly fastened, through fear of robbers), and so I knew that he could not see the opening of the door, and I kept pushing it on steadily, steadily.

I had my head in, and was about to open the lantern, when my thumb slipped upon the tin latch, and the old man sprang up in bed, crying out—"Who's there?"

I kept quite still and said nothing. For a whole hour I did not move a muscle, and in the meantime I did not hear him lie down. He was still sitting up in the bed listening—just as I have done, night after night, hearkening to the death-watches in the wall.

Presently I heard a slight groan, and I knew it was the groan of mortal terror. It was not a groan of pain or grief—oh, no!—it was the low stifled sound that arises from the bottom of the soul when overcharged with awe. I knew the sound well. Many a night, just at midnight, when all the world slept, it has welled up from my own bosom, deepening, with its dreadful echo, the terrors that distracted me. I say I knew it well. I knew what the old man felt, and pitied him, although I chuckled at heart. I knew that he had been lying awake ever since the first slight noise, when he had turned in the bed. His fears had been ever since growing upon him. He had been trying to fancy them causeless, but could not. He had been saying to himself—"It is nothing but the wind in the chimney—it is only a mouse crossing the floor," or "It is merely a cricket which has made a single chirp." Yes, he h   as been trying to comfort himself with these suppositions; but he had found all in vain. *All in vain;* because Death, in approaching him, had stalked with his black shadow before him, and enveloped the victim. And it was the mournful influence of the unperceived shadow that caused him to feel—although he neither saw nor heard—to *feel* the presence of my head within the room.

When I had waited a long time, very patiently, without hearing him lie down, I resolved to open a little—a very, very little crevice in the lantern. So I opened it— you cannot imagine how stealthily, stealthily—until, at length, a single dim ray, like the thread of the spider, shot from out the crevice and fell full upon the vulture eye.

It was open—wide, wide open—and I grew furious as I gazed upon it. I saw it with perfect distinctness—all a dull blue, with a hideous veil over it that chilled the very marrow in my bones; but I could see nothing else of the old man's face or person, for I had directed the ray, as if by instinct, precisely upon the damned spot.

"The Tell-Tale Heart" by Edgar Allan Poe, continued

And now—have I not told you that what you mistake for madness is but over-acuteness of the senses?—now, I say, there came to my ears a low, dull, quick sound, such as a watch makes when enveloped in cotton. I knew *that* sound well too. It was the beating of the old man's heart. It increased my fury, as the beating of a drum stimulates the soldier into courage.

But even yet I refrained and kept still. I scarcely breathed. I held the lantern motionless. I tried to see how steadily I could maintain the ray upon the eye. Meantime, the . . . tattoo of the heart increased. It grew quicker and quicker, and louder and louder every instant. The old man's terror must have been extreme! It grew louder, I say, louder every moment!—do you mark me well? I have told you that I am nervous; so I am. And now at the dead hour of night, amid the dreadful silence of that old house, so strange a noise as this excited me to uncontrollable terror. Yet, for some minutes longer I refrained and stood still. But the beating grew louder, louder! I thought the heart must burst. And now a new anxiety seized me—the sound would be heard by a neighbor! The old man's hour had come! With a loud yell, I threw open the lantern and leaped into the room. He shrieked once—once only. In an instant I dragged him to the floor, and pulled the heavy bed over him. I then smiled gaily, to find the deed so far done. But, for many minutes, the heart beat on with a muffled sound. This, however, did not vex me; it would not be heard through the wall. At length it ceased. The old man was dead. I removed the bed and examined the corpse. Yes, he was stone, stone dead. I placed my hand upon the heart and held it there many minutes. There was no pulsation. He was stone dead. His eye would trouble me no more.

Stop and Record

Make some notes in the "Middle" section of the Story Organizer (page 123).

If still you think me mad, you will think so no longer when I describe the wise precautions I took for the concealment of the body. The night waned, and I worked hastily, but in silence. First of all I dismembered the corpse. I cut off the head and the arms and the legs.

I then took up three planks from the flooring of the chamber, and deposited all between the crossbeams. I then replaced the boards so cleverly, so cunningly, that no human eye—not even *his*—could have detected anything wrong. There was nothing to wash out—no stain of any kind—no blood-spot whatever. I had been too wary for that. A tub had caught all—ha! ha!

When I had made an end of these labors, it was four o'clock—still dark as midnight. As the bell sounded the hour, there came a knocking at the street door. I

Fiction

"The Tell-Tale Heart" by Edgar Allan Poe, continued

went down to open it with a light heart—for what had I *now* to fear? There entered three men, who introduced themselves, with perfect politeness, as officers of the police. A shriek had been heard by a neighbor during the night, suspicion of foul play had been aroused; information had been lodged at the police station, and they (the officers) had been deputed to search the premises.

I smiled—for *what* had I to fear? I bade the gentlemen welcome. The shriek, I said, was my own in a dream. The old man, I mentioned, was vacationing in the country. I took my visitors all over the house. I bade them search—search *well*. I led them, at length, to his chamber. I showed them his treasures, secure, undisturbed. In the enthusiasm of my confidence, I brought chairs into the room, and desired them *here* to rest from their fatigues, while I myself, in the wild audacity of my perfect triumph, placed my own seat upon the very spot beneath which reposed the corpse of the victim.

The officers were satisfied. My *manner* had convinced them. I was singularly at ease. They sat, and while I answered cheerily, they chatted familiar things. But, ere long, I felt myself getting pale and wished them gone. My head ached, and I fancied a ringing in my ears; but still they sat and still chatted. The ringing became more distinct;—it continued and became more distinct; I talked more freely to get rid of the feeling; but it continued and gained explicitness—until, at length, I found that the noise was not within my ears.

No doubt I now grew *very* pale;—but I talked more fluently, and with a heightened voice. Yet the sound increased—and what could I do? It was *a low, dull, quick sound— much like a sound a watch makes when enveloped in cotton.* I gasped for breath—and yet the officers heard it not. I talked more quickly—more vehemently; but the noise steadily increased. I arose and argued about trifles, in a high key and with violent gesticulation; but the noise steadly increased. Why *would* they not be gone? I paced the floor to and fro with heavy strides, as if excited to fury by the observation of the men—but the noise steadily increased. Oh, God! what *could* I do? I foamed—I raved—I swore. I swung the chair upon which I had been sitting, and grated it upon the boards, but the noise arose over all and continually increased. It grew louder—louder—*louder!* And still the men chatted pleasantly, and smiled. Was it possible they heard not? Almighty God—no, no! They heard!—they suspected!—they *knew!*—they were making a *mockery* of my horror!—this I thought, and this I think. But anything was better than this agony! Anything was more tolerable than this derision! I could bear those hypocritical smiles no longer! I felt that I must scream or die!—and now—again!— hark! louder! louder! louder! *louder!*—

"Villains!" I shrieked, "pretend no more! I admit the deed!—tear up the planks!— here, here!—it is the beating of his hideous heart!"

Stop and Record
Make some notes in the "End" section of the Story Organizer (page 123).

 **Plan**

Next make a plan. Since your purpose is to find out what happens in the story, the strategy of using graphic organizers can help.

• Graphic organizers can keep you focused and on track as you read.

During Reading

Now go back and do a careful reading of Poe's story. Use the Story Organizer below for your notes.

D **Read with a Purpose**

Keep your reading purpose in mind. Remember that you need to ask and answer questions about the story.

Directions: Make notes on this organizer as you read.

Story Organizer

Beginning	Middle	End
What happens?	What happens?	What happens?
Where does it happen?	Where does it happen?	Where does it happen?
Which characters are involved?	Which characters are involved?	Which characters are involved?

Fiction

Using the Strategy

All different kinds of graphic organizers work well with short stories. Use the one that works best for you or the one that works best with the story you're reading.

• **Graphic organizers help you track, process, and remember important details from a text.**

Directions: Record details about "The Tell-Tale Heart" on this Fiction Organizer.

Fiction Organizer

Author's name
Title
Characters
Who they are . . .
What I know about them . . .
Setting
Time . . .
Place . . .
Plot
What happens first . . .
What happens next . . .
What happens after that . . .
At the end . . .

NAME ....

Understanding How Stories Are Organized

The plots of many short stories can be divided into five basic parts: exposition, rising action, climax, falling action, and resolution.

Directions: Use this Plot Diagram to show the organization of "The Tell-Tale Heart." See page 309 of your handbook if you need help.

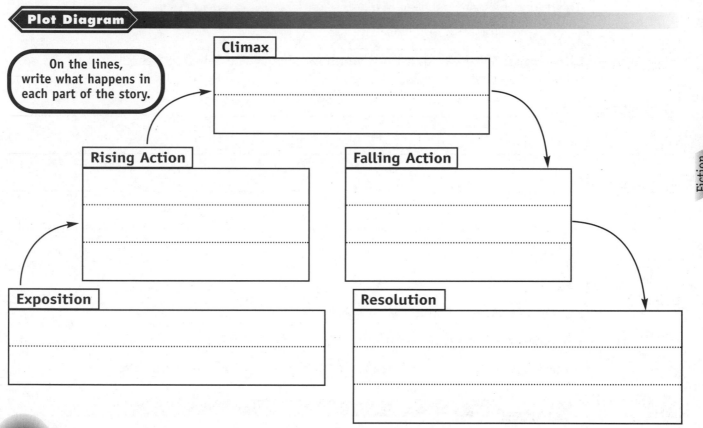

Plot Diagram

On the lines, write what happens in each part of the story.

Climax

Rising Action

Falling Action

Exposition

Resolution

E Connect

When you read a story, explore your own reactions to it. This can enhance your enjoyment of the work.

• **Recording how a story made you feel can help you make a connection to the reading.**

Directions: Reread the last paragraph of "The Tell-Tale Heart." Then record how the ending made you feel.

The ending made me feel ....

....

....

....

Fiction

After Reading

Many short stories will leave you with questions. This is because good writing hints at possibilities and suggests ideas.

F **Pause and Reflect**

What questions are you left with after reading the story?

• **After you finish a story, ask yourself, "How well did I meet my purpose?"**

Directions: Write two questions you have about "The Tell-Tale Heart."

My question: _____

_____

My question: _____

_____

 Reread

Rereading can help you answer lingering questions.

• **A powerful rereading strategy to use is close reading.**

Directions: Look at these lines from Poe's story. Write your reactions.

Double-entry Journal

Text of "The Tell-Tale Heart"	What I Think about It
"Whenever it fell upon me, my blood ran cold; and so by degrees—very gradually—I made up my mind to take the life of the old man, and thus rid myself of the eye forever."	
"In an instant I dragged him to the floor, and pulled the heavy bed over him. I then smiled gaily, to find the deed so far done."	
"'Villains!' I shrieked, 'no more! I admit the deed!—tear up the planks!—here, here!—it is the beating of his hideous heart!'"	

NAME ....

 Remember

Good readers remember what they've read.

• To remember a story, try making the information your own.

Directions: Write a journal entry about "The Tell-Tale Heart." Say what you did and didn't like about the story, and support it with good details.

Journal Entry

"The Tell-Tale Heart" by Edgar Allan Poe

Fiction

Reading a Novel

Novels can take you to places you've never been, to times long past or far into the future. The key to reading a novel is staying focused and paying attention to what happens.

Before Reading

Practice reading and responding to a novel here. Use the reading process and the strategy of synthesizing to help you get more from Mark Twain's novel, *The Adventures of Tom Sawyer.*

A Set a Purpose

When reading a novel for an assignment, your purpose is to understand the major literary elements of the book: *character, setting, plot, dialogue,* and *style.*

• **To set your purpose, ask important questions about the major elements of the novel.**

Directions: You will be reading a selection from Chapter 6 of *The Adventures of Tom Sawyer.* What will be your purpose for reading? Write your questions about the major elements below.

Purpose Chart

Element	My Questions
characters	Who are the major characters?
setting	Where does it take place?
plot	Whats the story about?
dialogue	Is there a conflict?
style	How does the author tell the story?

B Preview

A quick preview of a novel can help you know what to expect during your careful reading.

Directions: Preview the front and back covers of *The Adventures of Tom Sawyer*. Write important information on the sticky notes.

Back Cover

Meet one of the most unforgettable characters in world literature: the irrepressible, rascally, and wildly funny Tom Sawyer . . .

Mark Twain is the pseudonym of Samuel Langhorne Clemens. Clemens was born on November 30, 1835, in Florida, Missouri, and grew up in Hannibal, Missouri, on the west bank of the Mississippi.

To write his world-famous novel *The Adventures of Tom Sawyer*, Clemens looked back on the days of his childhood in Hannibal and the rough-and-tumble pranks that he and his friends pulled, all in the name of good fun.

If you enjoy this book about the willful Tom Sawyer, be sure to read its sequel, *The Adventures of Huckleberry Finn*—yet another classic by Mark Twain.

Front Cover

The Adventures of TOM SAWYER
BY Mark Twain

The title:

The Adventures of Tom Sawyer

The author:

Mark Twain a.k.a. Samuel L. Clemens

Information about the author:

Mark Twain is not his real name

Information about the book:

It's about his past

 **Plan**

Once your preview is done, choose a strategy that can help you explore the elements of plot, setting, character, dialogue, and style.

• **Use the strategy of synthesizing to understand various literary elements and how they work together in a novel.**

<u>Directions:</u> Make notes on this Fiction Organizer as you read *The Adventures of Tom Sawyer*.

Fiction Organizer

Characters Who are they?

Tom Sawyer ; Sid ; Aunt Polly

What are they like?

adventerous ;

Setting Where and when does the story take place?

On a Monday morning

The Adventures of Tom Sawyer

Plot What happens?

He's done something wrong that hurt his aunt.

Dialogue What do the characters say?

Good and bad things not that great of stuff.

Style What do you notice about Twain's writing style?

There's plenty of dialgoue

During Reading

D Read with a Purpose

Completing a Fiction Organizer as you read can help you stay focused on your purpose.

Directions: Think about characters, setting, plot, dialogue, and style as you read.

---

from *The Adventures of Tom Sawyer* by Mark Twain

MONDAY morning found Tom Sawyer miserable. Monday morning always found him so—because it began another week's slow suffering in school. He generally began that day with wishing he had had no intervening holiday, it made the going into captivity and fetters again so much more odious.

Tom lay thinking. Presently it occurred to him that he wished he was sick; then he could stay home from school. Here was a vague possibility. He canvassed his system. No ailment was found, and he investigated again. This time he thought he could detect colicky symptoms, and he began to encourage them with considerable hope. But they soon grew feeble, and presently died wholly away. He reflected further. Suddenly he discovered something. One of his upper front teeth was loose. This was lucky; he was about to begin to groan, as a "starter," as he called it, when it occurred to him that if he came into court with that argument, his aunt would pull it out, and that would hurt. So he thought he would hold the tooth in reserve for the present, and seek further. Nothing offered for some little time, and then he remembered hearing the doctor tell about a certain thing that laid up a patient for two or three weeks and threatened to make him lose a finger. So the boy eagerly drew his sore toe from under the sheet and held it up for inspection. But now he did not know the necessary symptoms. However, it seemed well worthwhile to chance it, so he fell to groaning with considerable spirit.

Stop and Record
Make notes in the "Setting" section of the Fiction Organizer (page 130).
Where and when does the story take place?

from *The Adventures of Tom Sawyer,* continued

But Sid slept on unconscious.

Tom groaned louder, and fancied that he began to feel pain in the toe.

No result from Sid.

Tom was panting with his exertions by this time. He took a rest and then swelled himself up and fetched a succession of admirable groans.

Sid snored on.

Tom was aggravated. He said, "Sid, Sid!" and shook him. This course worked well, and Tom began to groan again. Sid yawned, stretched, then brought himself up on his elbow with a snort, and began to stare at Tom. Tom went on groaning.

Sid said:

"Tom! Say, Tom!" [No response.] "Here, Tom! TOM! What is the matter, Tom?" And he shook him and looked in his face anxiously.

Tom moaned out: "Oh, don't, Sid. Don't joggle me."

"Why, what's the matter, Tom? I must call auntie."

"No—never mind. It'll be over by and by, maybe. Don't call anybody."

"But I must! DON'T groan so, Tom, it's awful. How long you been this way?"

"Hours. Ouch! Oh, don't stir so, Sid, you'll kill me."

"Tom, why didn't you wake me sooner? Oh, Tom, DON'T! It makes my flesh crawl to hear you. Tom, what is the matter?"

"I forgive you everything, Sid. [Groan.] Everything you've ever done to me. When I'm gone—"

"Oh, Tom, you ain't dying, are you? Don't, Tom—oh, don't. Maybe—"

"I forgive everybody, Sid. [Groan.] Tell 'em so, Sid. And Sid, you give my window-sash and my cat with one eye to that new girl that's come to town, and tell her—"

But Sid had snatched his clothes and gone. Tom was suffering in reality, now, so handsomely was his imagination working, and so his groans had gathered quite a genuine tone.

Sid flew downstairs and said: "Oh, Aunt Polly, come! Tom's dying!"

Stop and Record

Make notes in the "Characters" section of the Fiction Organizer (page 130). Which characters are important to this part of the novel?

"Dying!"

"Yes'm. Don't wait—come quick!"

"Rubbage! I don't believe it!"

But she fled upstairs, nevertheless, with Sid and Mary at her heels. And her face grew white, too, and her lip trembled. When she reached the bedside she gasped out:

from *The Adventures of Tom Sawyer,* continued

"You, Tom! Tom, what's the matter with you?"

"Oh, auntie, I'm—"

"What's the matter with you—what is the matter with you, child?"

"Oh, auntie, my sore toe's mortified!"

Stop and Record

Make notes in the "Plot" section of the Fiction Organizer (page 130).
What is Tom doing, and why is he doing it?

The old lady sank down into a chair and laughed a little, then cried a little, then did both together. This restored her and she said: "Tom, what a turn you did give me. Now you shut up that nonsense and climb out of this."

The groans ceased and the pain vanished from the toe. The boy felt a little foolish, and he said: "Aunt Polly, it SEEMED mortified, and it hurt so I never minded my tooth at all."

"Your tooth, indeed! What's the matter with your tooth?"

"One of them's loose, and it aches perfectly awful."

"There, there, now, don't begin that groaning again. Open your mouth. Well—your tooth IS loose, but you're not going to die about that. Mary, get me a silk thread, and a chunk of fire out of the kitchen."

Tom said: "Oh, please, auntie, don't pull it out. It don't hurt any more. I wish I may never stir if it does. Please don't, auntie. I don't want to stay home from school."

"Oh, you don't, don't you? So all this row was because you thought you'd get to stay home from school and go a-fishing? Tom, Tom, I love you so, and you seem to try every way you can to break my old heart with your outrageousness."

By this time the dental instruments were ready. The old lady made one end of the silk thread fast to Tom's tooth with a loop and tied the other to the bedpost. Then she seized the chunk of fire and suddenly thrust it almost into the boy's face. The tooth hung dangling by the bedpost, now.

Stop and Record

Make notes in the "Dialogue" and "Style" sections of the Fiction Organizer (page 130).
What is the tone of Twain's writing?

Fiction

Using the Strategy

The strategy of synthesizing can help you zero in on one or more literary elements.

• Use the strategy of synthesizing to analyze a novel's dialogue.

Dialogue is the conversations carried on between characters in a work of fiction. Dialogue can provide important clues about the characters.

Directions: Read the quotations in the first column. Then make inferences about the characters based on what they say. Record your inferences in the second column.

Double-entry Journal

Quote	My Inferences
" 'Tom, why didn't you wake me sooner? Oh, Tom, DON'T! It makes my flesh crawl to hear you. Tom, what is the matter?' "	Tom is being yelled at
" 'Aunt Polly, it SEEMED mortified, and it hurt so I never minded my tooth at all.' "	Tom is telling much about his tooth.
" 'Oh, please, auntie, don't pull it out. It don't hurt any more. I wish I may never stir if it does. Please don't, auntie. I don't want to stay home from school.' "	His aunt is pulling his teeth out or tooth.
"' Oh, you don't, don't you? So all this row was because you thought you'd get to stay home from school and go a-fishing? Tom, Tom, I love you so, and you seem to try every way you can to break my old heart with your outrageousness.' "	His aunt find's out the truth

Understanding How
Novels Are Organized

Most plots progress in chronological (time) order.

• Use a Story String to keep track of the events of a plot.

Directions: Use this organizer to show the series of events that happen in the reading from *The Adventures of Tom Sawyer*.

Story String

1. Tom checks his body for aches and pains.

▼

2. He tells Sid

▼

3. They find out about his tooth

▼

4. he tells his aunt

▼

5. his aunt tries to pull it out

▼

6. He confesses the truth to his aunt

Fiction

E Connect

Making connections to a novel can increase your enjoyment and understanding of the work.

• To make a connection, compare yourself to a character.

Directions: Complete this Venn Diagram. Write details about yourself and Tom in the large circles. Use the center section to tell what you have in common.

Venn Diagram

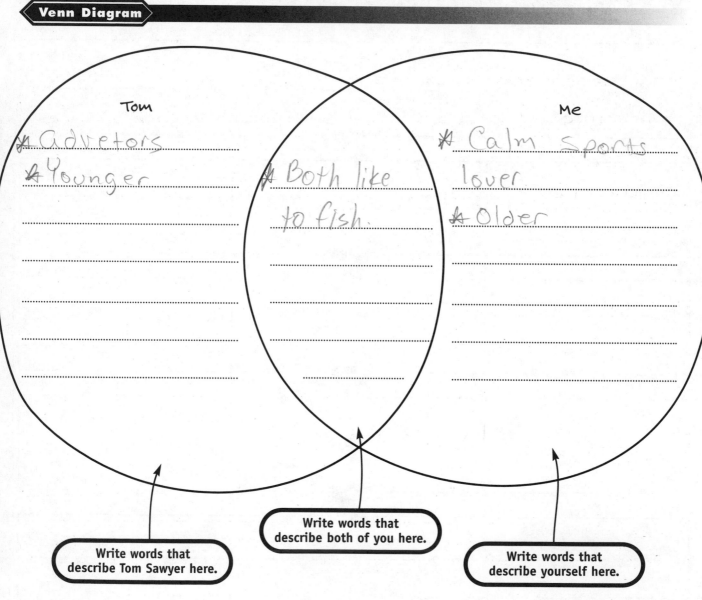

Tom
* Advetors
* Younger

* Both like
to fish.

Me
* Calm sports
lover
* Older

Write words that
describe Tom Sawyer here.

Write words that
describe both of you here.

Write words that
describe yourself here.

After Reading

When you finish a novel, take a few minutes to process what you've learned. Once again, the strategy of synthesizing can help.

F Pause and Reflect

Think about the major elements of the novel.

• **At this point, ask yourself: "How well did I meet my purpose?"**

Directions: Use the Web to ask yourself questions about how the elements work in *The Adventures of Tom Sawyer*. You can refer to page 336 in your handbook. Answer your questions. One is done for you.

Web

Can I describe the setting? This part of the novel takes place in Tom's and Sid's bedroom in Aunt Polly's house.

Is the diagloues spooken righe? The diaglove is in the right order.

Is the plot tell you something? It shows me not to lie

The Adventures of Tom Sawyer

are the charcters are important? Most of but there is only 3 main ones Tom, Sid, Polly

Was the book worth reading? It was good I liked the lesson it taught.

Fiction

Reread

When you reread, focus on one or more of the literary elements. Create a graphic organizer that can help you keep track of what you discover.

• **Use graphic organizers to process information from a novel.**

<u>Directions:</u> Think about Tom Sawyer. Write what you know about him on this Character Map.

Character Map

What he says and does

He tells a lie
So he says his
tooth hurts

What others think about him

His aunt Polly
Sid care about
him.

(Tom Sawyer)

How he feels about others

He doesn't want
to hurt them

How I feel about him

Inspirational
but does the
wrong thing.

NAME _____

 Remember

Good readers remember the most important parts of a novel.

● **Evaluating a novel can help you remember it.**

Directions: Rate the reading from *The Adventures of Tom Sawyer*. Then explain.

Rate the Novel

Plot

1	2	③	4	5	6	7	8	9	10
Dull				Interesting				Very interesting	

Characters

1	2	3	4	5	6	⑦	8	9	10
Not believable			Somewhat believable				Very believable		

Setting

1	2	3	4	⑤	6	7	8	9	10
Not developed			Somewhat developed				Well developed		

Dialogue

1	2	3	4	5	6	7	⑧	9	10
Not believable			Somewhat believable				Very believable		

Style

1	2	3	4	5	6	7	8	⑨	10
Not engaging			Somewhat engaging				Very engaging		

Why I gave the ratings I did:

I thought the story was told interesting. A good lesson was taught

Focus on Characters

Understanding a story's main character or characters can help you understand the plot, theme, and minor characters in the work. Follow these steps to analyze a main character.

Step 1: Note what the character says and does.

Directions: Read this excerpt from the novel *I Am the Cheese*. Highlight what the narrator *does*. Underline what he *thinks about*.

from *I Am the Cheese* by Robert Cormier

I am riding the bicycle and I am on Route 31 in Monument, Massachusetts, on my way to Rutterburg, Vermont, and I'm pedaling furiously because this is an old-fashioned bike, no speeds, no fenders, only the warped tires and the brakes that don't always work and the handlebars with cracked rubber grips to steer with. A plain bike—the kind my father rode as a kid years ago. It's cold as I pedal along, the wind like a snake slithering up my sleeves and into my jacket and my pants legs, too. But I keep pedaling, I keep pedaling. . . .

It's ten o' clock in the morning and it is October, not a Thomas Wolfe October of burning leaves and ghost winds but a rotten October, dreary, cold, and damp with little sun and no warmth at all. Nobody reads Thomas Wolfe anymore, I guess, except my father and me. I did a book report on *The Web and the Rock* and Mr. Parker in English II regarded me with suspicion and gave me a B- instead of the usual A. But Mr. Parker and the school and all that are behind me now and I pedal. Your legs do all the work on an old bike like this, but my legs feel good, strong, with staying power. I pass by a house with a white picket fence and I spot a little kid who's standing on the sidewalk and he watches me go by and I wave to him because he looks lonesome and he waves back.

I look over my shoulder but there's no one following.

NAME ....

Step 2: Organize.

Next, create an organizer that shows what you've learned about the character.

Directions: List what you know so far about the narrator of Cormier's novel.

Character Web

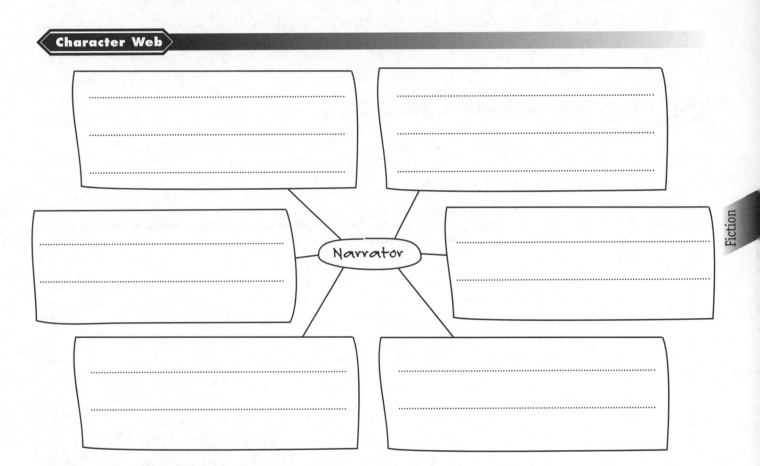

Step 3: Make inferences.

Finish by making inferences (reasonable guesses) about the character.

Directions: Complete this Inference Chart. Name two qualities or "traits" of the narrator. Then write your inferences based on the text.

Inference Chart

Traits of Narrator	What I Can Conclude

Focus on  Setting

Setting is where and when the action of a story takes place. It can affect the mood, characters, and plot of a story. Follow these steps to analyze a setting.

Step 1: Do a close reading.

Directions: Read this excerpt from "To Build a Fire." Highlight clues about time of day. Underline clues about place. Use the setting chart to keep track of the setting clues you found.

from "To Build a Fire" by Jack London

Day had broken cold and gray, exceedingly cold and gray, when the man turned aside from the main Yukon trail and climbed the high earth-bank, where a dim and little-traveled trail led eastward through the fat spruce timberland. It was a steep bank, and he paused for breath at the top, excusing the act to himself by looking at his watch. It was nine o'clock. There was no sun nor hint of sun, though there was not a cloud in the sky. It was a clear day, and yet there seemed an intangible pall over the face of things, a subtle gloom that made the day dark, and that was due to the absence of sun. This fact did not worry the man. He was used to the lack of sun. It had been days since he had seen the sun, and he knew that a few more days must pass before that cheerful orb, due south, would just peep above the skyline and dip immediately from view.

Step 2: Organize important details.

Use a chart to keep track of the various clues you find about time and place.

Directions: Complete this Setting Chart for "To Build a Fire."

Setting Chart

Clues about time	Clues about place
time of day:	where the story takes place:
season:	

Step 3: Draw conclusions about the mood.

Often the setting will help establish the mood, or atmosphere, of a story. Happiness, sadness, and peacefulness are examples of moods you will find in stories.

Directions: In the left column, write an example from the text that shows the setting. In the right column, write your thoughts about the mood created by the choice of setting.

Double-entry Journal

Quote	My Thoughts about the Mood

Step 4: Draw conclusions about the characters.

Watch how the main character reacts to the setting. The character's reaction can give you clues about his or her personality.

Directions: Complete this chart.

Inference Chart

The setting makes the man feel . . .	My inferences about him . . .

Fiction

Focus on Dialogue

When reading dialogue, pay attention to who is speaking, what is being said, and how it is being said. Follow these steps when analyzing dialogue.

Step 1: Do a careful reading.

First, read the dialogue slowly and carefully. Think about who is talking, what the two people are saying, and how they are saying it.

Directions: Read this excerpt from *Dicey's Song*. Write your notes.

from *Dicey's Song* by Cynthia Voigt

Dicey leaned her bike up against the grimy plate glass window and entered the dim little store. Millie was at the back, leaning against the top of the meat counter. "What can I do for you today?" she asked. "Your grandmother forget something?" Her little blue eyes rested lazily on Dicey. She had gray hair braided into circles around her head.

"No," Dicey answered. "I came to ask you if you might give me a job."

"A job? Why? Why should I do that? I don't make enough to keep myself in comfortable shoes," Millie told her.

"But if I kept the place cleaner, more people would want to come and shop," Dicey argued. "If I washed the windows and the floors and dusted off the shelves and the cans and the boxes."

"My Herbie used to do that," Millie said, "before he died. Business isn't good," she told Dicey.

Dicey made herself be patient. She'd just been talking about that, and how to make it better. "But it should be," she argued. She'd thought about this on the bike ride into town. "I mean, you have the only grocery store right downtown, the only store that people can walk to. The supermarkets are way out on the edge of town, and people have to drive there. It would be more convenient for people to come to you. If your store looked nicer they would want to."

Who is talking?

What are the two people saying?

How are they saying it?

Step 2: Look for clues about character.

Ask yourself, "What does the dialogue reveal about each character?"

Directions: Use a Double-entry Journal to record interesting dialogue and make inferences about the characters.

Double-entry Journal

Quotes	My thoughts

Step 3: Look for clues about plot.

As a next step, think about the story's plot. Dialogue can provide clues about what's going to happen next.

Directions: Predict what you think will happen next in *Dicey's Song*. Then explain your prediction.

My prediction: ....

My explanation: ....

Step 4: Look for clues about mood.

What the characters say and how they say it can affect a story's mood.

Directions: Fill in the following information. What is the mood of this scene from *Dicey's Song*? Which character or characters help create this mood?

Mood: Character who creates it:

....

Fiction

Focus on  Plot

Plot is the series of events that connects the beginning of a story to the end. Follow these steps to analyze the plot of a story or novel.

Step 1: Track key events.

In a well-written plot, one event leads into another, like stairs on a staircase.

Directions: Read these events from the myth "King Midas." Then number them in the correct order and draw sketches on the Storyboard that reflect the action.

Events:

_____ Sure he will starve, Midas asks to have the gift taken away.

_____ The god Bacchus offers Midas a gift, anything he might wish for.

_____ Midas finds to his dismay that the food he touches turns to gold as well.

_____ Midas is thrilled with his newfound power.

_____ Bacchus tells Midas to wash away his greed and its punishment in the river.

_____ Midas asks that anything he touches might be turned into gold, and Bacchus consents.

Storyboard

1.	2.	3.
4.	5.	6.

Step 2: Analyze the conflict.

Next, think about the central conflict in the work.

Directions: Read a passage from "King Midas." Then, explain the story's central conflict.

from "King Midas" by Thomas Bulfinch

Midas went his way, rejoicing in his new-acquired power, which he hastened to put to the test. He could scarce believe his eyes when he found a twig of an oak, which he plucked from the branch, became gold in his hand. He took up a stone; it changed to gold. He touched a sod; it did the same. He took an apple from the tree; you would have thought he had robbed the garden of Hesperides. His joy knew no bounds, and as soon as he got home, he ordered the servants to set a splendid repast on the table. Then he found to his dismay that whether he touched bread, it hardened in his hand; or put a morsel to his lip, it defied his teeth. He took a glass of wine, but it flowed down his throat like melted gold.

The conflict:

....

....

....

....

....

Fiction

Step 3: Think about the theme.

Quite often, the events of a plot can reveal the writer's theme.

Directions: Read more from "King Midas." Then write the myth's topic, details, and theme on the organizer.

from "King Midas" by Thomas Bulfinch

He raised his arms, all shining with gold, in prayer to Bacchus, begging to be delivered from his glittering destruction. Bacchus, merciful deity, heard and consented. "Go," said he, "to the River Pactolus, trace the stream to its fountain-head, there plunge in your head and body, and wash away your fault and its punishment."

Topic and Theme Organizer

Topic: ....

Detail #1:
....
....
....

Detail #2:
....
....
....

Detail #3:
....
....
....

Theme: ....
....
....
....

Focus on

Theme is the writer's message, or main idea, in a work of fiction. Your job is to find the clues about theme and figure out what they mean. This three-step plan can help.

Step 1: Find the "big ideas" in the work.

Sometimes the title, the first paragraph, or the background information will give you a clue about the author's "big ideas," or general topics.

Directions: Read this introduction, title, and first few lines from a well-known book. Write what you think some general topics will be.

This classic tale takes place in a fictional small town in Missouri, along the banks of the Mississippi River. Tom Sawyer is a boy who is always getting into mischief, and his active imagination leads him to be a bit of a liar, too. Tom lives with Aunt Polly. Although he is usually a trial for her, he often makes her smile.

"Tom!"
No answer.
"Tom!"
No answer.
"What's gone with that boy, I wonder? You TOM!"

General topics: ....

....

....

Fiction

Step 2: Consider what the characters do or say that relates to the "big ideas."

Next, make a connection between the characters and the "big ideas" in the work.

Directions: Read these lines from *The Adventures of Tom Sawyer*. Tell how they relate to the "big ideas" you noted earlier.

Double-entry Journal

Quote	What I Think about It
"Presently it occurred to him that he wished he was sick; then he could stay home from school."	
"Tom was suffering in reality, now, so handsomely was his imagination working, and so his groans had gathered quite a genuine tone."	
The old lady sank down into a chair and laughed a little, then cried a little, then did both together. This restored her and she said: "Tom, what a turn you did give me. Now you shut up that nonsense and climb out of this."	

Step 3: Decide on the author's message.

Remember that theme is the point the author wants to make about the topic.

Directions: Use the information from Steps 1 and 2 to complete this organizer.

Topic and Theme Organizer

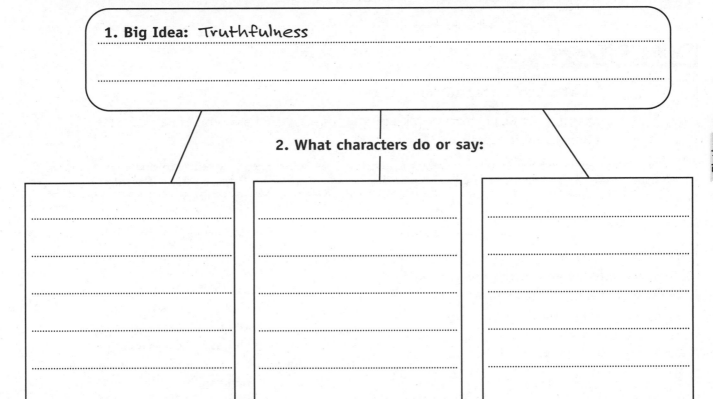

1. Big Idea: Truthfulness

2. What characters do or say:

3. What is important to learn:

Focus on Comparing and Contrasting

When you make a specific comparison, you compare one literary element in two works. For example, you might compare two settings or two characters. Follow these steps to make a specific comparison.

Step 1: Read.

As a first step, read and take notes.

Directions: Read these novel excerpts. Highlight clues about time. Underline clues about place.

from *Summer of the Monkeys* by Wilson Rawls	from *The Pearl* by John Steinbeck

It was the late 1800s, the best I can remember. Anyhow—at the time, we were living in a brand-new country that had just been opened up for settlement. The farm we lived on was called Cherokee land because it was smack dab in the middle of the Cherokee Nation. It lay in a strip from the foothills of the Ozark Mountains to the banks of the Illinois River in northeastern Oklahoma. This was the last place in the world that anyone would expect to find a bunch of monkeys.

. . . Kino got up and wrapped his blanket about his head and nose and shoulders. He slipped his feet into his sandals and went outside to watch the dawn.

Outside the door he squatted down and gathered the blanket ends about his knees. He saw the specks of Gulf clouds flame high in the air. And a goat came near and sniffed at him and stared with its cold yellow eyes. Behind him Juana's fire leaped into flame and threw spears of light through the chinks of the brush-house wall and threw a wavering square of light out the door. A late moth blustered in to find the fire. The Song of the Family came now from behind Kino. And the rhythm of the family song was the grinding stone where Juana worked the corn for the morning cakes.

Step 2: Organize.

Next, organize what you know about the element to be compared.

Directions: Complete this Setting Chart.

Setting Chart

Novel	Clues about time	Clues about place
Summer of the Monkeys		
The Pearl		

Step 3: Draw conclusions.

Use a Venn Diagram to compare and contrast the two elements.

Directions: Complete this Venn Diagram.

Venn Diagram

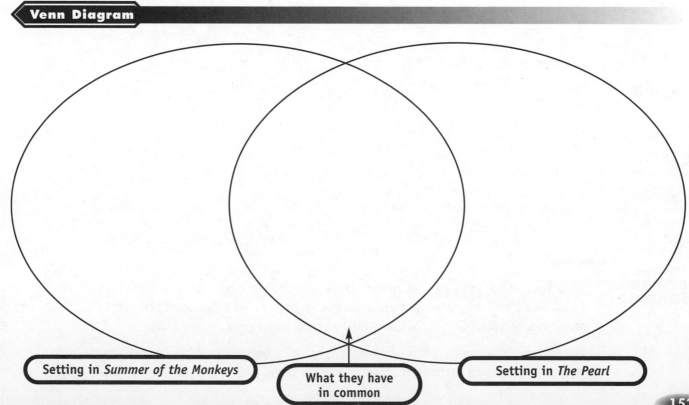

Setting in *Summer of the Monkeys*   What they have in common   Setting in *The Pearl*

Fiction

Reading a Poem

Good readers of poetry look for meaning, listen for sounds, and visualize a poem's images. They follow a plan that can help them get more from every poem they read.

Before Reading

Reading poetry takes time and patience. Practice using the reading process and the strategy of close reading with the classic poem "O Captain! My Captain!" by Walt Whitman.

A Set a Purpose

Your purpose for reading a poem is twofold: First, you need to find out what the poem is about; second, you need to figure out what it means.

- **To set your purpose, ask a question about the subject and meaning of the poem.**

Directions: Write your purpose for reading "O Captain! My Captain!" here. Then tell what you already know about the poet or the poem.

My purpose: ....

....

What I already know: ....

....

....

....

B Preview

As a first step, preview the poem. Look at the title and name of the poet. Read any explanatory text. Skim the poem and then read the first stanza carefully.

Directions: Preview "O Captain! My Captain!" Then make some notes. Use your notes to answer the questions on page 156.

Walt Whitman (1819–1892) is one of America's finest poets. One of his most famous poems, "O Captain! My Captain!" first appeared in his groundbreaking anthology of poetry, Leaves of Grass. *In this poem and others, Whitman reveals the love and admiration he felt for Abraham Lincoln, and the despair he felt upon hearing the news of his assassination.*

"O Captain! My Captain!"

by Walt Whitman

Preview Notes

The title: ....

The poet's name: ....

I learned this from the background information: ....

....

The subject: ....

I saw these repeated words: ....

....

Here's what I noticed about the shape and structure of the poem: ....

....

....

....

"O Captain! My Captain!" by Walt Whitman

O captain! my captain! our fearful trip is done;
The ship has weather'd every rack, the prize we sought is won;
The port is near, the bells I hear, the people all exulting,
While follow eyes the steady keel, the vessel grim and daring;
But O heart! heart! heart!
O the bleeding drops of red,
Where on the deck my captain lies,
Fallen cold and dead.

O captain! my captain! rise up and hear the bells;
Rise up—for you the flag is flung—for you the bugle trills;
For you bouquets and ribbon'd wreaths—for you the shores a-crowding;
For you they call, the swaying mass, their eager faces turning;
Here captain! dear father!
This arm beneath your head;
It is some dream that on the deck,
You've fallen cold and dead.

My captain does not answer, his lips are pale and still;
My father does not feel my arm, he has no pulse nor will;
But the ship is anchor'd safe, its voyage closed and done;
From fearful trip the victor ship comes in with object won:
Exult, O shores, and ring, O bells!
But I with mournful tread,
Walk the deck my Captain lies,
Fallen cold and dead.

1. Who or what is the subject of this poem?

2. What is the rhythm of this poem? What does it sound like?

3. What is the mood and tone of "O Captain! My Captain!"?

C Plan

After your preview, choose a reading strategy that you think will work well with the text.

• Use the strategy of close reading with poetry.

If you can, plan to read a poem more than once. This will help you relax because you won't try to think about everything all at one time.

During Reading

D Read with a Purpose

On your first reading of a poem, read for enjoyment. On your second reading, read for meaning. On your third reading, read for structure and tone.

Directions: Read Whitman's poem three times. After each reading, make some notes on this chart.

Plan for Reading a Poem

First Reading	Second Reading	Third Reading
Here's what I liked about the poem:	I think Whitman's message is this:	Here's what I noticed about the rhyme: rhythm: tone:

Poetry

FOR USE WITH PAGES 408–421

Using the Strategy

Close reading means reading word for word, line by line. To use the strategy, create a Double-entry Journal.

• **A Double-entry Journal can help you respond to individual lines in a poem.**

Directions: Read the lines from Whitman's poem in the left column. Write what you think the words mean or how they make you feel in the right column.

Double-entry Journal

Quote	My Thoughts and Feelings
"But O heart! heart! heart! O the bleeding drops of red"	
"For you bouquets and ribbon'd wreaths —for you the shores a-crowding; For you they call, the swaying mass, their eager faces turning; Here captain! dear father!"	
Write an important or interesting line from the poem here. Then write how it makes you feel.	

© GREAT SOURCE. ALL RIGHTS RESERVED.

Understanding How Poems Are Organized

It's important that you understand the choices the poet makes
in organizing a poem. The strategy of close reading can help.

Directions: Reread Whitman's poem. Then complete the sticky notes.

"O Captain! My Captain!" by Walt Whitman

O captain! my captain! our fearful trip is done;
The ship has weather'd every rack, the prize we sought is won;
The port is near, the bells I hear, the people all exulting,
While follow eyes the steady keel, the vessel grim and daring;
 But O heart! heart! heart!
  O the bleeding drops of red,
   Where on the deck my captain lies,
    Fallen cold and dead.

O captain! my captain! rise up and hear the bells;
Rise up—for you the flag is flung—for you the bugle trills;
For you bouquets and ribbon'd wreaths—for you the shores a-crowding;
For you they call, the swaying mass, their eager faces turning;
 Here captain! dear father!
  This arm beneath your head!
   It is some dream that on the deck,
    You've fallen cold and dead.

My captain does not answer, his lips are pale and still;
My father does not feel my arm, he has no pulse nor will;
But the ship is anchor'd safe, its voyage closed and done;
From fearful trip the victor ship comes in with object won:
 Exult, O shores, and ring, O bells!
  But I with mournful tread,
   Walk the deck my Captain lies,
    Fallen cold and dead.

I noticed this about
the number and
length of the stanzas:

....

....

....

Poetry

I noticed these
rhyming words:

....

....

....

The poem uses figurative
language to compare

....

....

to ....

....

E Connect

Making a personal connection to a word, line, or stanza can strengthen your understanding and enjoyment of the poem.

> **• Record how the poem makes you feel.**

Directions: Think about "O Captain! My Captain!" Then tell how Whitman's words made you feel.

When I read the poem, I felt:

_____

_____

Here's why:

_____

Here's how the speaker of the poem feels about Lincoln's death:

_____

Here's how I know this:

_____

_____

After Reading

Before you leave a poem, take the time to figure out what you know.

F Pause and Reflect

At this point, you'll want to return to your reading purpose. When you finish a poem, ask yourself: "How well did I meet my purpose?"

Directions: Circle *have* or *have not*. Then explain your answer.

I feel I have / have not met my reading purpose. Here's why:

_____

_____

Reread

Use the rereading strategy of paraphrasing to focus on particular lines in the poem—perhaps the ones you liked best or the ones you didn't understand.

• **A powerful rereading strategy to use with poetry is paraphrasing.**

<u>Directions:</u> Read the lines in the first column. Write paraphrases of the lines in the second column.

Paraphrase Chart

Lines	My Paraphrase
"But the ship is anchor'd safe and sound, its voyage closed and done; From fearful trip, the victor ship comes in with object won . . ."	

 Remember

Good readers remember the overall message of a poem.

• **Making a sketch can help you remember a poem's subject and message.**

<u>Directions:</u> Make a sketch of "O Captain! My Captain!" Then write a caption that explains what you've drawn.

Journal Sketch

caption:

Poetry

Focus on Language

Language is part of what makes poetry so rich. Most poets use few words, but they know how to make every word count. Follow these steps to analyze the language of a poem.

Step 1: Read and take notes.

First, read the poem all the way through without stopping. Then read it a second time. Highlight words and phrases that catch your attention.

Directions: Read "The Eagle," a famous poem by Alfred, Lord Tennyson. Underline words that grab your attention.

"The Eagle" by Alfred, Lord Tennyson

> He clasps the crag with crooked hands;
> Close to the sun in lonely lands,
> Ring'd with the azure world, he stands.
>
> The wrinkled sea beneath him crawls;
> He watches from his mountain walls,
> And like a thunderbolt he falls.

Step 2: Find key words.

Next, read the poem again. Watch for key words, including words that describe an action, create a mood, or name a person, place, or thing.

Directions: Reread "The Eagle," one line at a time. Highlight the two most important words in each line and write them in the left column. Write your ideas in the right column.

◄ **Two Per Line** ►

Words   **My Ideas**

....

....

....

....

....

....

Step 3: Look for figurative language and imagery.

Finish your analysis by looking for figurative language and imagery in the poem.

Directions: Find examples of simile, alliteration, and imagery in "The Eagle." Check "Elements of Poetry" (pages 446–469) if you need help with these terms.

Simile (a comparison using *like* or *as*)	**Alliteration** (repetition of sounds)	**Imagery** (words that appeal to the five senses)
Example:	Example:	Example:

Focus on Meaning

When you read a poem, it's natural to try and figure out what it means. Use the reading process and the strategy of close reading to help you focus on meaning.

Step 1: Read for the subject.

As a first step, read the poem all the way through without stopping. Try to get an idea of what it is about.

Directions: Read this sonnet by Elizabeth Barrett Browning. Make notes.

"Sonnet" by Elizabeth Barrett Browning

How do I love thee? Let me count the ways.
I love thee to the depth and breadth and height
My soul can reach, when feeling out of sight
For the ends of being and ideal grace.
I love thee to the level of every day's
Most quiet need, by sun and candlelight.
I love thee freely, as men strive for right;
I love thee purely, as they turn from praise.
I love thee with the passion put to use
In my old griefs, and with my childhood's faith.
I love thee with a love I seemed to lose
With my lost saints,—I love thee with the breath,
Smiles, tears, of all my life!—and, if God choose,
I shall but love thee better after death.

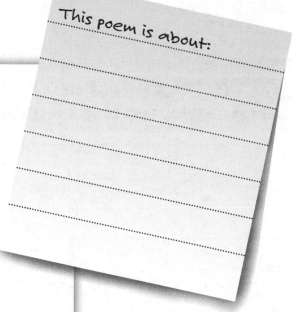

This poem is about:

Here are my inferences about the speaker of the poem:

Step 2: Consider what's unusual and important.

Next, reread the poem line by line. Look for unusual and important words.

Directions: Write important lines from the poem in this Double-entry Journal. Then write your thoughts as you make sense of the lines.

Double-entry Journal

Important Lines	My Thoughts

Step 3: Explore your feelings.

Think about your personal response to the poem.

Directions: Answer these questions. Refer to your notes as needed.

What did you picture when you were reading the poem? ....

....

How do Browning's words make you feel? ....

....

Step 4: Decide what the poet is saying.

Finish by considering what the poet is trying to say. What is the message for readers? This formula can help.

Directions: Use the formula to write about the poem.

Topic of the poem   +   **what the poet is saying about the topic =   poem's message**

....

....   **+**   ....   **=**   ....

....

Poetry

Focus on Sound and Structure

Understanding the sound and structure can increase your enjoyment in reading a poem or song. Follow these steps.

Step 1: Do a careful reading.

Begin by reading all the way through without stopping. Then take a moment to examine how the lines look on the page.

Directions: Read these lines from a song. Write what you notice on the sticky notes.

"Swing Low, Sweet Chariot," Author Unknown

I ain't never been to heaven but I been told,
Comin' for to carry me home,
That the streets in heaven are paved with gold,
Comin' for to carry me home.

Swing low, sweet chariot,
Comin' for to carry me home,
Swing low, sweet chariot,
Comin' for to carry me home.

I noticed this about the words:

I noticed this about the way the lines are grouped:

I noticed this about the punctuation:

Step 2: Look for repeated words and sounds.

Next, listen to the "music" of the lines. What do the words *sound* like?

Directions: Reread the lines. Highlight repeated words, and underline repeated sounds. Write what you noticed on this chart.

Chart	
Examples of Repeated Words	**Examples of Repeated Sounds**
swing low	

Step 3: Listen for rhyme.

Analyzing the rhyme scheme can further your understanding of the poem. You can use letters to show the rhyme pattern.

Directions: Return to "Swing Low, Sweet Chariot." Use letters to show the rhyme scheme. Write the letters next to the first four lines. Refer to pages 442–443 in your handbook if you need help.

Step 4: Listen for rhythm.

Review the definition for rhythm on page 463 of your handbook. Can you hear a rhythm or "beat" in "Swing Low, Sweet Chariot"?

Directions: Whisper the lines to yourself. Write four lines of the poem below and mark the syllables that are stressed, or accented. See page 463 in your handbook.

....

....

....

....

....

Reading a Play

The entire action of a play is revealed through dialogue and stage directions. When you read a play, you need to listen to what the characters say and visualize what the characters see.

Before Reading

Practice reading a play here. Use the reading process and the strategy of summarizing to help you get more from these lines from a play called *Trifles*.

 A ## Set a Purpose

Your purpose for reading a play is to find out about the four major elements of drama.

• **To set your purpose, ask a question about the setting, characters, conflict, and theme of the play.**

Directions: Write your purpose for reading *Trifles* here. Then tell what the word *trifles* means to you.

My purpose: ....

....

....

....

To me, the word *trifles* means: ....

....

....

....

NAME

B Preview

When you preview a play, pay attention to any introductory material, including the title page and cast of characters.

• **Previewing a play helps you know what to expect during your careful reading.**

Directions: Preview the title page and first several lines from *Trifles* (page 170). Write your preview ideas on the sticky notes.

The play has

act.

The title is

Trifles

A play in one act

by Susan Glaspell

First Performed by the Provincetown Players at the Wharf Theatre, Provincetown, Massachusetts, on August 8, 1916

Cast of Characters

GEORGE HENDERSON, County Attorney

HENRY PETERS, Sheriff

LEWIS HALE, A Neighboring Farmer

MRS. PETERS

MRS. HALE

There are

main characters.

The setting is

Setting

TIME: early 1900s

PLACE: a farmhouse in the middle of the country

Act 1, Scene 1

Here's what I noticed:

Drama

from *Trifles* by Susan Glaspell

(SCENE: *The kitchen in the now abandoned farmhouse of* JOHN WRIGHT. *It is a gloomy kitchen, and left without having been put in order—unwashed pans under the sink, a loaf of bread outside the bread box, a dishtowel on the table—and other signs of incomplete work. At the rear, the outer door opens and the* SHERIFF *comes in followed by the* COUNTY ATTORNEY *and* MR. HALE. *The* SHERIFF *and* HALE *are men in middle life, the* COUNTY ATTORNEY *is a young man; all are much bundled up and go at once to the stove. They are followed by the two women—the* SHERIFF'S WIFE *first; she is a slight wiry woman, a thin nervous face.* MRS. HALE *is larger and would ordinarily be called more comfortable looking, but she is disturbed now and looks fearfully about as she enters. The women have come in slowly, and stand close together near the door.*)

Stop and Organize

Fill in the "Setting" box of your Fiction Organizer (page 174).

COUNTY ATTORNEY *(Rubbing his hands)*: This feels good. Come up to the fire, ladies.

MRS. PETERS *(After taking a step forward)*: I'm not—cold.

SHERIFF *(Unbuttoning his overcoat and stepping away from the stove as if to mark the beginning of official business)*: Now, Mr. Hale, before we move things about, you explain to Mr. Henderson just what you saw when you came here yesterday morning.

COUNTY ATTORNEY: By the way, has anything been moved? Are things just as you left them yesterday?

SHERIFF *(Looking about)*: It's just the same. When it dropped below zero last night I thought I'd better send Frank out this morning to make a fire for us—no use getting pneumonia with a big case on, but I told him not to touch anything except the stove—and you know Frank.

COUNTY ATTORNEY: Somebody should have been left here yesterday.

SHERIFF: Oh—yesterday. When I had to send Frank to Morris Center for that man who went crazy—I want you to know I had my hands full yesterday. I knew you could get back from Omaha by today and as long as I went over everything here myself—

from _Trifles_ by Susan Glaspell, continued

COUNTY ATTORNEY: Well, Mr. Hale, tell just what happened when you came here yesterday morning.

HALE: Harry and I had started to town with a load of potatoes. We came along the road from my place and as I got here I said, "I'm going to see if I can't get John Wright to go in with me on a party telephone." I spoke to Wright about it once before and he put me off, saying folks talked too much anyway, and all he asked was peace and quiet—I guess you know about how much he talked himself; but I thought maybe if I went to the house and talked about it before his wife, though I said to Harry that I didn't know as what his wife wanted made much difference to John—

COUNTY ATTORNEY: Let's talk about that later, Mr. Hale. I do want to talk about that, but tell now just what happened when you got to the house.

Stop and Organize

Fill in the "Characters" box of your Fiction Organizer (page 174).

HALE: I didn't hear or see anything; I knocked at the door, and still it was all quiet inside. I knew they must be up, it was past eight o'clock. So I knocked again, and I thought I heard somebody say, "Come in." I wasn't sure, I'm not sure yet, but I opened the door—this door _(Indicating the door by which the two women are still standing)_ and there in that rocker—_(Pointing to it)_ sat Mrs. Wright.

(They all look at the rocker.)

COUNTY ATTORNEY: What—was she doing?

HALE: She was rockin' back and forth. She had her apron in her hand and was kind of—pleating it.

COUNTY ATTORNEY: And how did she—look?

HALE: Well, she looked strange.

COUNTY ATTORNEY: How do you mean—strange?

HALE: Well, as if she didn't know what she was going to do next. And kind of done up.

COUNTY ATTORNEY: How did she seem to feel about your coming?

Drama

from *Trifles* by Susan Glaspell, continued

HALE: Why, I don't think she minded—one way or other. She didn't pay much attention. I said, "How do, Mrs. Wright, it's cold, ain't it?" And she said, "Is it?"—and went on kind of pleating at her apron. Well, I was surprised; she didn't ask me to come up to the stove, or to set down, but just sat there, not even looking at me, so I said, "I want to see John." And then she—laughed. I guess you would call it a laugh. I thought of Harry and the team outside, so I said a little sharp: "Can't I see John?" "No," she says, kind o' dull like. "Ain't he home?" says I. "Yes," says she, "he's home." "Then why can't I see him?" I asked her, out of patience. " 'Cause he's dead," says she. "Dead?" says I. She just nodded her head, not getting a bit excited, but rockin' back and forth. "Why—where is he?" says I, not knowing what to say. She just pointed upstairs—like that *(Himself pointing to the room above)*. I got up, with the idea of going up there. I walked from there to here—then I says, "Why, what did he die of?" "He died of a rope round his neck," says she, and just went on pleatin' at her apron. Well, I went out and called Harry. I thought I might—need help. We went upstairs and there he was lyin'—

COUNTY ATTORNEY: I think I'd rather have you go into that upstairs, where you can point it all out. Just go on now with the rest of the story.

HALE: Well, my first thought was to get that rope off. It looked . . . *(Stops, his face twitches)* . . . but Harry, he went up to him, and he said, "No, he's dead all right, and we'd better not touch anything." So we went back downstairs. She was still sitting that same way. "Has anybody been notified?" I asked. "No," says she, unconcerned. "Who did this, Mrs. Wright?" said Harry. He said it businesslike—and she stopped pleatin' of her apron. "I don't know," she says. "You don't *know?*" says Harry. "No," says she. "Weren't you sleepin' in the bed with him?" says Harry. "Yes," says she, "but I was on the inside." "Somebody slipped a rope round his neck and strangled him and you didn't wake up?" says Harry. "I didn't wake up," she said after him. We must 'a looked as if we didn't see how that could be, for after a minute she said, "I sleep sound." Harry was going to ask her more questions but I said maybe we ought to let her tell her story first to the coroner, or the sheriff, so Harry went fast as he could to Rivers' place, where there's a telephone.

Stop and Organize

Fill in the "Plot" box of your Fiction Organizer (page 174).

from *Trifles* by Susan Glaspell, continued

COUNTY ATTORNEY: And what did Mrs. Wright do when she knew that you had gone for the coroner?

HALE: She moved from that chair to this one over here *(Pointing to a small chair in the corner)* and just sat there with her hands held together and looking down. I got a feeling that I ought to make some conversation, so I said I had come in to see if John wanted to put in a telephone, and at that she started to laugh, and then she stopped and looked at me—scared. . . .

(The COUNTY ATTORNEY, *who has had his notebook out, makes a note.)*

HALE *(Continuing)*: I dunno, maybe it wasn't scared. I wouldn't like to say it was. Soon Harry got back, and then Dr. Lloyd came, and you, Mr. Peters, and so I guess that's all I know that you don't.

COUNTY ATTORNEY *(Looking around)*: I guess we'll go upstairs first—and then out to the barn and around there. *(To the* SHERIFF*)* You're convinced that there was nothing important here—nothing that would point to any motive.

SHERIFF: Nothing here but kitchen things.

(The COUNTY ATTORNEY, *after again looking around the kitchen, opens the door of a cupboard closet. He gets up on a chair and looks on a shelf. Pulls his hand away, sticky.)*

COUNTY ATTORNEY: Here's a nice mess.

(The women draw nearer.)

MRS. PETERS *(To the other woman)*: Oh, her fruit; it did freeze. *(To the* COUNTY ATTORNEY*)* She worried about that when it turned so cold. She said the fire'd go out and her jars would break.

SHERIFF: Well, can you beat the women! Held for murder and worryin' about her preserves.

COUNTY ATTORNEY: I guess before we're through she may have something more serious than preserves to worry about.

HALE: Well, women are used to worrying over trifles.

Drama

Plan

After you preview, make a plan. Choose a strategy that can help you explore the setting, characters, plot, and theme of the play. Summarizing as you read is a good way to keep track of what happens, where it happens, and who says what.

• **Use the strategy of summarizing to help you meet your purpose.**

During Reading

D Read with a Purpose

Be sure to keep your reading purpose in mind as you read.

Directions: Now go back and do a careful reading of *Trifles*. Make notes on the Fiction Organizer below. Save the theme box for later.

Fiction Organizer

Characters	Setting

Title

Plot	Theme

Using the Strategy

When you summarize a play, you tell the events of the plot in your own words.

• **Summarizing can help you process and remember what you've read.**

Directions: Summarize the scene you've just read from *Trifles*. Write your notes on this organizer.

Summary Notes

Write what you think is the main point or idea here.

....

....

List three or four smaller, related points that support the main idea here.

1. ....

....

....

2. ....

....

....

3. ....

....

....

4. ....

....

....

Drama

Understanding How
Plays Are Organized

A play is always organized around a central conflict. The conflict is the main problem the characters must solve.

• To fully understand a play, you must examine the central conflict.

Directions: Make notes about the conflict in *Trifles*. Then predict how you think things will turn out.

The conflict:

_____

_____

_____

Here's how I predict the problem will be solved:

_____

_____

_____

E Connect

Making a personal connection to a play can help you understand the playwright's theme, or message.

• Imagining yourself a part of a scene can help you uncover the theme of a play.

Directions: Tell how you would feel if you were there in the room with Mr. Hale and the others.

I would feel

_____

_____

because

_____

_____

_____

After Reading

When you finish reading, think about the play's big ideas.

F Pause and Reflect

Reflect on the major topics of the play. Record your ideas on an organizer.

• Use a graphic such as a Magnet Summary to organize your thoughts about a play's big ideas.

Directions: Read the "big idea" in the center of the Magnet Summary. Then, in the circles, write details from the play that relate to this idea.

Magnet Summary

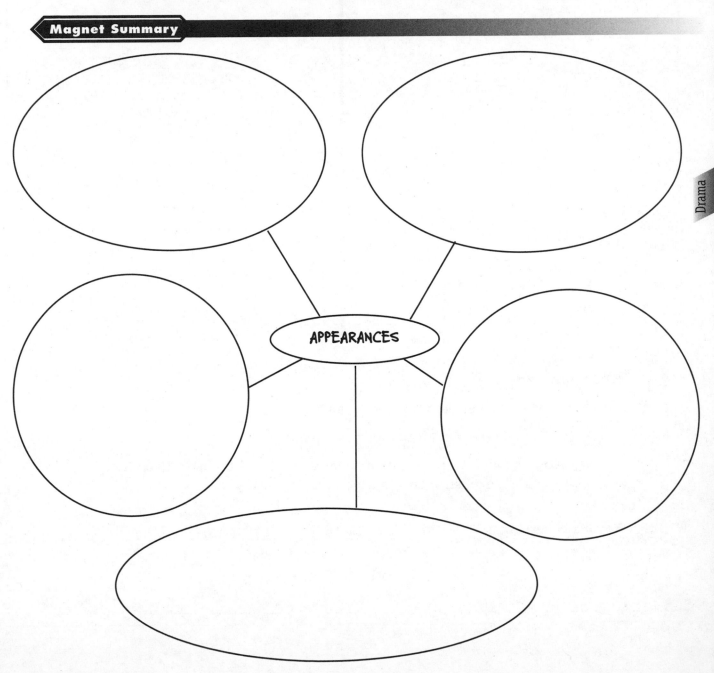

APPEARANCES

Drama

 Reread

If you're not sure of a play's themes, you'll need to return to the text. Choose a reading tool that can help you get more from your rereading.

• Visualizing can help you "see" what happens in a play.

<u>Directions:</u> Sketch two scenes from the play. Show the characters and what they are doing. Then make some notes on the lines.

Storyboard

1.	2.

....
....
....

H Remember

Good readers remember what they've read.

• To remember a play, focus on a key passage.

<u>Directions:</u> Skim *Trifles*. Highlight what you think is the most important passage. Then explain why it is important.

<u>Why this passage is important:</u> ....
....
....

Focus on Theme

In most cases, a play will have a major theme and one or more minor themes. Follow these steps to find a play's themes.

Step 1: Find the "big ideas" or general topics.

Begin by asking yourself, "What are some of the play's general topics?"

Directions: List two general topics in *Trifles*. Write them here.

General Topics in *Trifles*

Topic #1:_____ _____	Topic #2:_____ _____

Drama

Step 2: Note what the characters do or say that relates to the general topics.

Next, think about the relationship between the characters and the general topics.

Directions: Tell what the characters in *Trifles* do and say that relates to the two general topics. Make notes here.

General Topic #1: Appearances	General Topic #2: Men's and women's views
What the characters do:	What the characters do:
What they say:	What they say:

Step 3: Write a statement of the author's point or message about a general topic.

Be careful not to confuse a play's topic with its theme. The **topic** is what the play is about. The **theme** is the playwright's *message* about the topic.

Example

Write a general topic here   What the playwright says about it   My theme statement

| Little things (trifles) | + | Don't be fooled by little things. | = | A major theme in <u>Trifles</u> is that little things can add up to something big. |

Directions: Use this formula to find another theme in *Trifles*. Write a short opinion statement about the theme you've identified. Explain how it makes you feel and whether or not you agree with the playwright's message.

Write a general topic here.   Write the playwright's message about the topic here.

_____   +   _____

Write a theme statement here.

= _____

_____

How I feel about it:

....

....

....

....

....

....

....

Drama

Focus on  Language

If you "listen" carefully to a playwright's language, you'll find clues about setting, character, and theme.

Step 1: Read the stage directions.

Stage directions can help you "see" the setting of a play.

Directions: Read these stage directions. Then sketch the scene.

(SCENE: *The kitchen in the now abandoned farmhouse of* JOHN WRIGHT. *It is a gloomy kitchen, looks like it has been left without having been put in order —unwashed pans under the sink, a loaf of bread outside the bread box, a dishtowel on the table—and other signs of incomplete work.*) from Trifles by Susan Glaspell

Sketch

Step 2: Analyze the dialogue.

The words characters use when speaking to each other can help you understand their personalities.

Directions: Read this dialogue from *Trifles*. Then make inferences about the County Attorney and Mrs. Hale.

> ### from *Trifles* by Susan Glaspell
>
> COUNTY ATTORNEY: *(With the gallantry of a young politician)* And yet, for all their worries, what would we do without the ladies? *(The women do not unbend. He goes to the sink, takes a dipperful of water from the pail, and pouring it into a basin, washes his hands. Starts to wipe them on the roller-towel, turns it for a cleaner place.)* Dirty towels! *(Kicks his foot against the pans under the sink)* Not much of a housekeeper, would you say, ladies?
>
> MRS. HALE *(Stiffly)*: There's a great deal of work to be done on a farm.
>
> COUNTY ATTORNEY: To be sure. And yet *(With a little bow to her)* I know there are some Dickson county farmhouses which do not have such roller towels. . . .
>
> MRS. HALE: Those towels get dirty awful quick. Men's hands aren't always as clean as they might be.
>
> COUNTY ATTORNEY: Ah, loyal to your sex, I see. But you and Mrs. Wright were neighbors. I suppose you were friends, too.
>
> MRS. HALE *(Shaking her head)*: I've not seen much of her of late years. I've not been in this house—it's more than a year.
>
> COUNTY ATTORNEY: And why was that? You didn't like her?
>
> MRS. HALE. I liked her well enough. Farmers' wives have their hands full, Mr. Henderson. And then—
>
> COUNTY ATTORNEY: Yes—?
>
> MRS. HALE *(Looking about)*: It never seemed a very cheerful place.

My inferences about the County Attorney: ....

....

My inferences about Mrs. Hale: ....

....

....

Drama

Step 3: Study key lines and speeches.

Studying key lines and speeches can help you figure out a play's theme.

Directions: Find details in this speech that support Glaspell's topic of appearances. Write them on the organizer. One has been done for you. Then write the important lesson about appearances you learned from the details.

from *Trifles* by Susan Glaspell

MRS. HALE. I wish you'd seen [Mrs. Wright] when she wore a white dress with blue ribbons and stood up there in the choir and sang. *(A look around the room.)* Oh, I wish I'd come over here once in a while! That was a crime! That was a crime! Who's going to punish that?

Topic and Theme Organizer

Topic:
Appearances

Detail #1:

Mrs. Wright wore a
fancy dress during
happier times.

Detail #2:

Detail #3:

Theme:

NAME ....

Reading a  Website

Not all websites give reliable information. As a critical reader, you must zero in on what's important and then decide whether or not that information is reliable.

Before Reading

Practice using the reading process and the strategy of reading critically to navigate a website about American history.

 A **Set a Purpose**

It's easy to get distracted when reading a website. To prevent this from happening, decide on your purpose *before* you visit the site.

• **To set your purpose, make a list of questions about the subject.**

<u>Directions:</u> Use this chart to write questions about what you want to find out.

Questions

What I Want to Know
1. What period in American history can I find out about on this site?
2.
3.

Internet

B Preview

When you arrive at the website, take a moment to survey what's there. Get a sense of what is offered before you begin clicking.

Directions: Preview the American history website. Check each item on this checklist. Make notes on what you find.

Preview Checklist	My Notes
❑ the name and overall look of the site	
❑ the main menu or table of contents	
❑ the source or sponsor of the site	
❑ the introduction to the site	
❑ images or graphics	
❑ links to other sites	

http://historytime.org/americanhistorya-z/page1.asp

American History from A to Z

History from A to Z is an Internet website for students, teachers, and researchers of American history. The site offers information on both major and minor events in American History from 1600 to the present. In addition, the site serves as a gateway to Internet resources and offers useful materials for teaching and learning about U.S. history.

 click here for MORE ON THIS SITE

Select below to browse by feature:

Voices of the past
Letters, poems, and journals by famous and not-so-famous Americans

Primary documents
Newspaper and magazine articles about historical events

American speeches
The most famous speeches in America

www.history
Links to other history sites on the Web

Students of history
Examples of student notes and research papers on the web

Teachers of history
Course syllabi, teacher resources, and more

Images of history
Pictures of America, past and present

Reference desk
Links to encyclopedias, dictionaries, and other reference materials on the Web

A project of the Center for American History, an affiliate of State University in Sunnyside, Texas. Dr. Janelle Richardson, Ph.D., of State University is director of this site. Direct your comments to Dr. Richardson at www.jrichardson@cah.com.

Last updated: October 2002

Internet

Plan

Next make a plan. Use the strategy of reading critically to help you get *more* from the website.

• **Reading critically means examining the information you're given and deciding whether or not it is reliable.**

During Reading

Begin by reading the main menu, which often runs along the left side of the site. Then let your eyes roam over the rest of the page.

Read with a Purpose

As you skim the web page, focus on finding answers to your purpose questions. Make notes on a Website Profiler. It can help you understand and evaluate the most important elements of the website.

Directions: Read the American history website carefully. Record your notes on this Website Profiler.

Website Profiler

Name	URL
Sponsor	Date
Point of view	Expertise
My reaction	

Using the Strategy

Reading critically means examining the website in small pieces, perhaps one frame at a time. Remember that not every link will be useful to your purpose.

- **When you read critically, you decide which links will help you meet your purpose.**

Directions: Make notes about the American history website on these Study Cards. Decide which links would be valuable to follow. Explain why.

Study Cards

Links I should follow:

Keep your notes in front of you as you link your way through the site.

How they relate to my purpose:

Internet

Understanding How
Websites Are Organized

A website really does look like a web. The "spokes" that reach out
from the center of the web are paths or "links" that you can follow.

Directions: Complete this Web. List three important links on the history
website. Predict what you think you'll find there.

"American History from A to Z"

Link

Link

Link

E Connect

To make a connection to a website, consider how you feel about the
information.

• **Be sure to think about whether the website was of use to you.**

Directions: Think of two websites you've visited recently. Explain your
opinion of each site and why you will or will not return.

Website #1

My opinion of it:

Why I would or would not return:

Website #2

My opinion of it:

Why I would or would not return:

After Reading

Take your time when doing research on the Internet. Gather your thoughts about one site before linking on to the next.

F Pause and Reflect

Recall your original purpose for visiting the site. Return to the questions you created and make notes about what you learned.

• **After you visit a website, ask yourself, "How well did I meet my purpose? What else do I need to find out?"**

<u>**Directions:**</u> Return to the questions on page 185. Tell what you have learned. Then explain what else you'd like to learn.

I learned this from the website:

....

....

....

I want to know more about this:

....

....

....

Links that can help:

....

....

....

G Reread

Occasionally you may need to return to a site to double-check a fact or detail. Once again, think carefully about whether the information on the site is reliable.

• **A powerful rereading strategy to use when checking for reliability is skimming.**

Internet

Directions: Skim the website. Then answer the "reliability" questions on the organizer.

Website Profiler

1. What is the source of the site?	2. What credentials does the site offer?	3. What is the purpose of the site?

4. When was the site last updated?	5. Are there any obvious errors on the site?

H Remember

Good Internet researchers remember what they've seen and learned.

• **Summary Notes can help you remember a website.**

Directions: Write a list of four main things you learned at the American history website. Refer to your During Reading notes and questions as needed.

Summary Notes

website: www.historytime.org

Four things I learned at this site:

1.

2.

3.

4.

NAME ....

Reading a Graphic

The words and visuals are equally important in a graphic. Both contain vital information about its subject and purpose. Follow this plan when reading a graphic.

Before Reading

Use the reading process and the strategy of paraphrasing to help you understand the most important elements of a graphic.

 A **Set a Purpose**

Your purpose for reading a graphic is to find answers to two general questions: "What is the graphic about?" and "What can it tell me?"

• **To set your purpose, ask two questions about the graphic.**

Directions: Write your purpose questions for reading a bar graph about changes in U.S. farmland acreage from 1985 to 2000. Then make a prediction.

Question 1: ....

....

....

Question 2: ....

....

....

I predict this graphic will show: ....

....

....

....

B Preview

When you preview a graphic, look at both the words and picture.

• A graphic's words and picture both offer important information.

Directions: Preview the bar graph below. Then make notes on the chart.

Changes in Acreage Used for Farming in U.S.

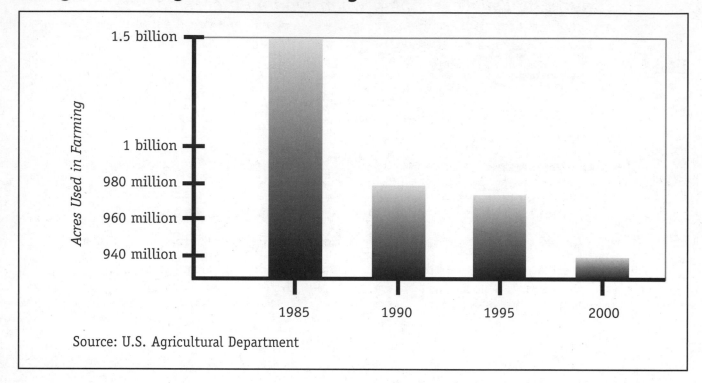

Source: U.S. Agricultural Department

The title of the bar graph is

The graphic shows

The source for the graphic is

NAME ....

C Plan

Next, choose a strategy that can help you interpret the graphic.

• The strategy of paraphrasing can help you get more from a graphic.

During Reading

Now do your careful reading. First look at the visual and decide what it shows. Then examine the text.

D Read with a Purpose

Keep your purpose questions in mind as you read. Make notes about information that relates to your two questions.

<u>Directions:</u> Read the bar graph on U.S. farmland acreage. Then paraphrase, or tell in your own words, what the graphic shows.

My Paraphrase

....

....

....

Graphics

Using the Strategy

Paraphrasing what you've learned in a graphic can help you process details and remember what you've learned.

• **Record your paraphrase and other important information on a Paraphrase Chart.**

Paraphrase Chart

My Paraphrase	
My Thoughts	
Connection	

Understanding How
Graphics Are Organized

Knowing the major elements of a graphic is key to unlocking its message.

Directions: Look at the graphic again. Label these parts: *title, source, horizontal* (x) *axis, and vertical* (y) *axis*. If needed, review the definitions for these terms on page 543 of your handbook.

Changes in Acreage Used for Farming in U.S.

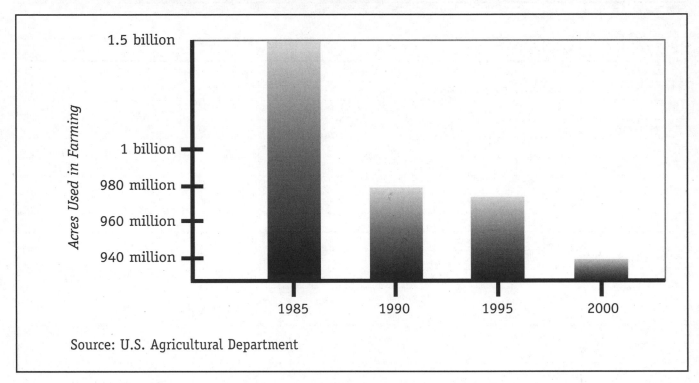

Source: U.S. Agricultural Department

Graphics

E Connect

Ask yourself, "What does this information mean to me?"

• **Use a Double-entry Journal organizer to record your personal response to a graphic.**

Directions: Write information from the bar graph in the first column. Then write your thoughts about the farmland graphic.

Double-entry Journal

GRAPHIC	MY THOUGHTS
U.S. Farmland Acreage	Most interesting:
	Most surprising:
	Most puzzling:

After Reading

Get into the habit of taking a second (or even a third) look at a graphic to be sure you haven't missed anything.

 Pause and Reflect

Think back to your reading purpose. Decide whether you've answered both of the questions you set out to answer.

• **Ask yourself, "How well did I meet my purpose?"**

Directions: Answer your reading purpose questions.

What is the graphic about?

....

....

What does it tell me?

....

....

Poetry

G Reread

Look again at the farmland bar graph. Ask yourself, "What conclusions can I draw?"

• **Use the rereading strategy of reading critically to help you draw conclusions about a graphic.**

Directions: Complete this chart. Refer to page 546 in your handbook if you get stuck.

Drawing Conclusions

Questions to Ask	Conclusions
1. What is being compared or classified?	
2. What similarities and differences in the data do you see?	
3. Is there anything unusual about the way the data is presented? Is anything left out?	
4. What trends or other relationships do you see?	

H Remember

It's easier to remember a graphic if you actually *do* something with the information.

• **To remember a graphic, make a list of key facts and details.**

Directions: Make a list of facts and details you learned from the farmland graphic.

Things I learned about farmland in the U.S.

1. _____

2. _____

Reading a Test and Test Questions

Tests are a necessary part of every student's life. Since there's no avoiding tests, you may as well do what you can to make taking them as easy and painless as possible. This plan can help.

Before Reading

After your teacher hands you the test, quickly set your purpose.

A Set a Purpose

For any test in any subject, your purpose is twofold. First, find out what the test questions are asking, and second, decide what information is needed to answer them.

• **To set your purpose, ask questions about the test.**

Directions: For this sample test, you'll read a passage from Roald Dahl's autobiography, *Boy: Tales of Childhood*. Write two reading purpose questions here.

My purpose questions: _____

_____

_____

_____

B Preview

After you set your purpose, preview the test. Try to get a sense of what is expected of you.

Directions: Skim the sample test that follows. Read the directions and take a quick look at the questions. Check each item on the checklist on page 203 as you preview.

Tests

Mid-year Reading Test

30 Minutes — 3 questions, 1 Essay

DIRECTIONS: Answer each question. Choose the correct answer and fill in the corresponding circle on your answer sheet. Write your essay in the blue test booklet.

Do not linger over questions that seem too difficult. Skip these and return to them later. You will not be penalized for incorrect answers.

MID-YEAR TEST, PASSAGE #1

"Captain Hardcastle"

In his autobiography, Roald Dahl describes people, places, and events that had an effect on him while he was growing up. As you read, try to get a sense of Dahl's opinion of his teacher, a man named Captain Hardcastle.

From *Boy: Tales of Childhood* by Roald Dahl

"Captain Hardcastle"

We called them masters in those days, not teachers, and at St. Peter's the one I feared most of all, apart from the Headmaster, was Captain Hardcastle.

This man was slim and wiry and he played football. On the football field he wore white running shorts and white gym shoes and short white socks. His legs were as hard and thin as a ram's legs and the skin around his calves was almost exactly the color of mutton fat. The hair on his head was not ginger. It was a brilliant dark vermilion, like a ripe orange, and it was plastered back with immense quantities of brilliantine in the same fashion as the Headmaster's. The parting in his hair was a white line straight down the middle of the scalp, so straight it could only have been made with a ruler. On either side of the parting you could see the comb tracks running back through the greasy orange hair like little tramlines.

Captain Hardcastle sported a mustache that was the same color as his hair, and oh what a mustache it was! A truly terrifying sight, a thick orange hedge that sprouted and flourished between his nose and his upper lip and ran clear across his face from the middle of one cheek to the middle of the other. . . .

Behind the mustache there lived an inflamed and savage face with a deeply corrugated brow that indicated a very limited intelligence. "Life is a puzzlement," the corrugated brow seemed to be saying, "and the world is a dangerous place. All men are enemies and small boys are insects that will turn and bite you if you don't get them first and squash them hard."

Mid-year Reading Test, continued

English: Mid-year Reading Test
MULTIPLE-CHOICE QUESTIONS

1. "Captain Hardcastle" is an example of what kind of writing?
   - ○ **A.** descriptive writing
   - ○ **B.** expository writing
   - ○ **C.** persuasive writing
   - ○ **D.** informational writing

2. Who was Captain Hardcastle?
   - ○ **A.** a boy
   - ○ **B.** a teacher
   - ○ **C.** a sailing instructor
   - ○ **D.** a headmaster

3. Hardcastle's expression seems to say, ". . . small boys are insects that will turn and bite you if you don't get them first and squash them hard." What does Dahl mean?
   - ○ **A.** Captain Hardcastle is not well liked by the boys or by the other masters.
   - ○ **B.** Small boys should not annoy the adults around them.
   - ○ **C.** Captain Hardcastle is a terrifying figure to the boys.
   - ○ **D.** Captain Hardcastle is funny to the boys, but he really fears them.

ESSAY QUESTION

4. Write an essay that tells how Roald Dahl feels about his former master. Support your opinion with facts and details from the passage.

Checklist
❏ How much time do you have to complete the test?
❏ What do you learn from the directions?
❏ Is there a penalty for guessing?
❏ What do you predict the reading will be about?
❏ What do you notice about the test questions?
❏ What does the essay question ask about?

Tests

C Plan

Many of the tests you take will contain a combination of factual recall and inference questions. What you need is a strategy that can help you correctly answer both types of questions.

- **Use the strategy of skimming to help you find answers to test questions.**

During Reading

Read the article, problem, or test item carefully before turning your attention to the questions.

D Read with a Purpose

Use a highlighter to mark important words and sentences in the passage or problem. This will save you time later, when you are looking for answers to the fact or recall questions.

Directions: Read the passage about Captain Hardcastle. Highlight the sentence mentioned in test question 3. What inference can you make about Hardcastle?

I think Dahl is saying that Hardcastle is
....

....

....

Using the Strategy

After you read a passage on a test, take a look at the questions. Read each one carefully. Then skim the reading for the answers.

- **Skim the passage for answers to the questions. Look for specific information that relates to the questions.**

Directions: Read the three multiple-choice test questions on page 203. Fill in the circles for the correct answers. Then explain your choices on the sticky notes.

How I figured out the answer to #1

How I figured out the answer to #2

How I figured out the answer to #3

Understanding How
Tests Are Organized

In many tests, the most challenging questions—those that require the most thought fall at the end.

Directions: Reread the essay question on page 203. Then explain which words and sentences in the reading give you clues about Dahl's attitude toward Captain Hardcastle.

Clues I found: ....

....

....

....

....

E Connect

The personal connections you make to a test passage can help you answer the open-ended questions.

• **Record your personal reactions to the person, place, or thing described.**

Directions: Write three or more words that describe Captain Hardcastle here. Then explain.

Captain Hardcastle is ....

....

and ....

Explanation: ....

....

....

....

....

After Reading

After you finish the test, take a moment to gather your thoughts.

F Pause and Reflect

Ask yourself, "Have I answered each question to the best of my ability?"

• **Return to the questions that gave you the most difficulty and double-check your answers.**

This is what I found most difficult in the passage:

....

....

....

Here are the three things I learned:

....

....

....

....

....

Here are two or three things I still need to learn more about:

....

....

....

....

....

....

....

....

Reread

You may need to do some rereading to help you with the more difficult passages and difficult questions.

• **A powerful rereading strategy to use is visualizing and thinking aloud.**

Directions: Write a Think Aloud that tells how you would answer the essay question. Refer to your During Reading notes as needed.

◄ **Think Aloud** ►

....

....

....

....

....

....

....

....

H Remember

Take a look at the test after your teacher has graded it.

• **Remember the test questions that gave you the most trouble. Similar questions may appear on future tests.**

Directions: Exchange books with a classmate. "Grade" each other's tests, and comment on the Think Alouds. Then write what *you* can do to improve your test-taking abilities.

I can improve my test-taking abilities by ....

....

....

....

....

Tests

Focus on Essay Tests

Here's a plan that can help you succeed on one of the more challenging types of tests you'll take as a student— the essay test.

Step 1: Preview.

As a first step, preview the directions and writing prompt. Underline key words and phrases.

Directions: Read the essay assignment and prompt. Underline key words and phrases. Then retell the assignment on the sticky note.

Sample Test

DIRECTIONS: Write an opinion essay about a proposed change in your school's curriculum. First read the prompt below. Then write your opinion statement. Next offer support for your opinion. Carefully proofread your writing when you've finished.

Prompt: Your school principal has announced that as a cost-cutting measure students will no longer have access to the Internet on school computers. How do you feel about this proposal? Write an essay stating your opinion. Support it with convincing evidence.

What I need to do to write this essay:

1.

2.

3.

Step 2: Organize.

It's extremely important that you take the time to organize your essay before you begin writing.

Directions: Use this Main Idea Organizer to plan your essay.

Main Idea Organizer

My Idea:		
Detail 1:	Detail 2:	Detail 3:
Concluding Sentence:		

Step 3: Write.

State your opinion in the introduction. Use the body of the essay to support your opinion.

Directions: Write the introductory paragraph for your essay here.

....

....

....

....

....

Step 4: Proofread.

Remember that errors can affect your score. Check for problems in spelling, punctuation, and usage.

Directions: Proofread and correct the paragraph you just wrote.

Tests

Focus on Vocabulary Tests

Vocabulary tests require knowledge of words and word parts. Follow these steps when taking a vocabulary test.

Step 1: Preview.

First skim the test to see what types of questions you'll be expected to answer. Highlight important words in each question.

Directions: Preview the two parts of this Sample Test. Highlight important words.

Sample Test

Part 1   DIRECTIONS: Choose the best synonym for the word.

1. GENIAL
   - ○ A. cordial
   - ○ C. unsociable
   - ○ B. talkative
   - ○ D. disagreeable

Part 2   DIRECTIONS: Choose an antonym for the word.

2. RIBALD
   - ○ A. rough
   - ○ C. refined
   - ○ B. slapstick
   - ○ D. hilarious

Step 2: Eliminate wrong answers.

First think about the word in the question. What do you know about this word or a part of it? Then read every choice, even if you're sure you know the answer. Cross out answers that are clearly *wrong*.

Directions: Look at questions 1 and 2 again. Cross out the answers you know are wrong.

Step 3: Solve analogies.

Save the analogies for last. To solve an analogy, first decide how the given word pair is related. Then choose another pair that has the same relationship.

Directions: Tell the relationship between the words *crumb* and *bread*. Then solve the analogies.

> ◆ **Sample Test** ◆
>
> 3. CRUMB : BREAD ::
>
>   ○ A. needle : pin   ○ B. splinter : wood
>
>   ○ C. cream : butter   ○ D. flower : vase
>
> 4. WRITE : RIGHT ::
>
>   ○ A. write : letter   ○ B. right : wrong
>
>   ○ C. their : there   ○ D. write : paper
>
> 5. CHICAGO : ILLINOIS ::
>
>   ○ A. Detroit : Michigan   ○ B. Los Angeles : San Francisco
>
>   ○ C. New York : Connecticut   ○ D. Florida : Miami

Step 4: Check.

Save a few minutes at the end of the test to check your work.

Directions: Answer the questions. Then compare answers with a classmate. If you disagree about an answer, explain your thinking.

Tests

Focus on Social Studies Tests

To do well on a social studies test, read the passages and test questions very carefully. Follow these steps to improve your score.

Step 1: Preview.

Quickly skim the test. Use a highlighter to mark familiar topics and concepts. Answer the easiest questions first.

Directions: Preview this Sample Test question. Highlight important words.

Sample Test

DIRECTIONS: Choose the best answer for each question.

1. Which of the following occurred as a result of the Spanish-American War of 1898?
   - ○ A. Cuba gained limited independence from Spain.
   - ○ B. The United States granted statehood to Puerto Rico.
   - ○ C. Franklin Delano Roosevelt was elected President of the United States.
   - ○ D. The United States formed an alliance with Germany and Russia.

Step 2: Rule out wrong answers.

Next, look for answers that you know are *wrong*.

Directions: Return to the test question. Cross out answers that you know are wrong. (Hint: Think about the *date* of the war. Why is C clearly wrong?)

Step 3: Reread the question.

Reread the question until you're sure you know what it's asking.

Directions: Tell what question #1 is asking you to figure out.

Question #1 wants me to figure out
....

....

....

Step 4: Talk your way through the possible answers.

Then use a Think Aloud for the remaining answers to the question.

Directions: Complete this Think Aloud.

▶ **Think Aloud**

I know that C is wrong because FDR was not elected President
....

in 1898. I also think   is wrong because
....

....

....

....

Step 5: Choose an answer and double-check.

Finally, choose an answer. Then reread the question to see if the answer makes sense.

Directions: Write what you think is the correct answer to the question. Then explain your choice.

My answer: ....

....

My explanation: ....

....

Tests

Focus on Math Tests

Math tests require your undivided attention. You'll need to use everything you know about numbers, concepts, and theories. Follow these steps to improve your score.

Step 1: Preview.

Always begin by previewing the test. Underline the most important information in each question.

Directions: Preview this Sample Question. Underline the most important parts.

> **Sample Question**
>
> **2.** Lila, Seth, and Carlos are to divide n books among them. If Lila receives twice as many books as Seth, and Carlos receives twice as many as Lila, how many books does Seth receive in terms of n?
>
> **A.** $\frac{n}{4}$ **C.** $\frac{n}{0}$
>
> **B.** $\frac{n}{7}$ **D.** $\frac{n}{12}$

Step 2: Eliminate wrong answers.

Whenever possible, use number sense to eliminate answers that are clearly *wrong*.

Directions: Return to the Sample Question. Cross out the answers that are clearly wrong. (Hint: One answer is too high and another is too low.)

Step 3: Estimate.

Always estimate the answer if you can. Doing some rough calculations may help you rule out another answer or two.

Directions: Look at the question again. How many books do you estimate Seth will receive?

I estimate he will receive _____ books.

Step 4: Think aloud.

Talk your way through the problem.

Directions: Complete this Think Aloud for the problem.

◄ Think Aloud ►

....
....
....
....
....
....
....

Step 5: Solve.

Write the numeric equation or expression that you can use to solve the problem. Then check to see that your answer is correct.

Directions: Look at the problem written as an equation. What is the correct answer?

$$x + 2x + 4x = \text{_____} x = n.$$

Answer: ....
....

Focus on Science Tests

During a science test, think like a scientist and use the scientific method. Follow these steps.

Step 1: Read.

First preview the test. Then read the individual test items and any graphics.

Directions: Read the table on this Sample Test. Complete the sticky notes.

The most deaths result from
.

Hurricanes

Hurricane Name	Date	Top Wind Speed (approx.)	Resulting Deaths	Damage to Property
Gilbert	1988	183 mph	318	$5 billion
Andrew	1992	180 mph	26	$25 billion
Hugo	1989	161 mph	49	$10 billion
Gabrielle	1989	144 mph	8	not known

Sample Test

DIRECTIONS: Read the table. Then answer questions 1 and 2.

1. What connection can you make between wind speed of a

   hurricane and loss of human life? ....

   ....

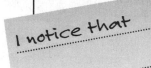

I notice that

2. Why do you suppose Hurricane Andrew caused five times as
   much damage to property as Gilbert?
   - ○ A. Housing prices changed dramatically from 1988 to 1992.
   - ○ B. Andrew hit a more heavily populated area.
   - ○ C. Slower wind speeds can actually cause more damage.
   - ○ D. All of the above.

216

Step 2: Read the questions.

Next, read the questions. Again, make notes as you go.

Directions: Read both questions and explain what you need to find out.

For Question #1, ...

For Question #2, ...

Step 3: Think Aloud.

Talk your way through possible answers to the questions.

Directions: Complete the Think Aloud.

◄ **Think Aloud**

Question #1 asks me to ....

....

....:

Question #2 asks me to ....

....

....:

Step 4: Check.

Check your answers by rewriting the questions as statements. Then check to see if the new statements are true.

Directions: Rewrite questions #1 and #2 from the Sample Test as statements.

Question #1 ....

....

Question #2 ....

....

Tests

Learning New Words

Words are something you want to collect, like designer T-shirts or video games. Follow these steps to "collect" new words and build your vocabulary.

Step 1: Read.

When you come to an unfamiliar word in your reading, don't just skip it— "collect" it.

Directions: Read this passage. Circle all unfamiliar words.

---

from *The Heart of a Woman* by Maya Angelou

I began to write. At first I limited myself to short sketches, then to song lyrics, then I dared short stories. When I met John Killens he had just come to Hollywood to write the screenplay for his novel *Youngblood*, and he agreed to read some of what he called my "work in progress." I had written and recorded six songs for Liberty Records, but I didn't seriously think of writing until John gave me his critique. After that I thought of little else. . . . John said, "Most of your work needs polishing. In fact, most of everybody's work could stand rewriting. But you have undeniable talent." He added, "You ought to come to New York. You need to be in the Harlem Writers Guild." The invitation was oblique but definitely alluring.

Step 2: Record.

Keep a list of "unknown" words in your vocabulary journal. Add to the list each time you read.

Step 3: Define.

Directions: Write the words you circled in the Maya Angelou passage on this journal page. You'll define them later.

◄ Vocabulary Journal ►

English

from The Heart of a Woman p.21

Unfamiliar words	Definitions

Step 4: Use.

The best way to remember a new word is to use it in conversation or writing.

Directions: Working with your partner, write one sentence for each word you defined.

◄ My Sentences ►

_____

_____

_____

_____

_____

_____

_____

Vocabulary

Building  Vocabulary

One way of building your vocabulary is to learn the technique of defining in context and some basic word families. Practice here.

Step 1: Use context clues.

What should you do if you come upon an unknown word and no dictionary is available? Try using context clues.

Directions: Review pages 615–620 in your handbook. Then read this excerpt. Use context clues to figure out the meaning of the underlined words. Make notes on the chart.

---

from "Olympic and Other Games" by Thomas Bulfinch

It seems not inappropriate to mention here the other celebrated national games of the Greeks. The first and most <u>distinguished</u> were the Olympic, founded, it was said, by Jupiter himself. They were celebrated at Olympia in Elis. <u>Vast</u> numbers of <u>spectators</u> flocked to them from every part of Greece, and from Asia, Africa, and Sicily. They were repeated every fifth year in midsummer and continued five days. They gave rise to the custom of <u>reckoning</u> time and dating events by Olympiads. The first Olympiad is generally considered as corresponding with the year *776* B.C.

Underlined Words	My Definition	Context Clues I Used
distinguished		
vast		
spectators		
reckoning		

NAME ....

Step 2: Use word parts.

Knowing various word parts, such as roots, prefixes, and suffixes can help you increase the number of new words you can understand.

Root Words

Directions: Complete this word tree. Add words that have the root *chron*.

chron

Prefixes

Directions: Add a prefix from the box to each of the words on the list. Then tell what the word means.

sub- = under	*neo-* = new	*anti-* = against

Prefix + Word	New Word	Meaning of New Word
1. + classic		
2. + merge		
3. + trust		

Suffixes

Directions: Add suffixes to these words. Then tell what you think the new word means.

-less = without	*-ence* = action, state of, quality of	*-some* = like, apt, tending to

base + -less = ... Meaning: ....

confer + -ence = ... Meaning: ....

motion + -less = ... Meaning: ....

lone + -some = ... Meaning: ....

Vocabulary

Dictionary Dipping

A dictionary is an indispensable tool for readers.

Step 1: Read.

Once you've found the entry you're looking for, carefully read the word's definition and make some notes.

Directions: Read the definitions for *malevolent* and *malfeasance*. Then answer the questions. See page 629 in your handbook if you get stuck.

> **Dictionary Dipping**
>
> **malevolent** (mə-lĕv′ə-lənt) *adj*. Having or exhibiting ill will; malicious. [from the Latin *malevolentia*.] —**malevolence** *n*. —**malevolently** *adv*.
>
> **malfeasance** (măl-fē′zəns) *n. Law*. Misconduct or wrongdoing, esp. by a public official. [from the Latin *malefacere*, do wrong.]

1. What part of speech is *malevolent?*
....

2. What is the adverbial form of *malevolent?*
....

3. What profession uses the word *malfeasance?*
....

4. What is the history of the word *malfeasance?*
....

Step 2: Remember.

The easiest way to remember a new word is to use it.

Directions: Write two sentences. Use *malevolent* in the first and *malfeasance* in the second.

Sentence #1: ....

....

Sentence #2: ....

Reading a Thesaurus

A thesaurus is a treasure chest of words. Unlocking the chest involves reading carefully and using what you learn.

Step 1: Read the entry.

Your purpose for reading a thesaurus is to find synonyms for a word. Begin by searching for an entry for the given word. Then read the synonyms listed.

Directions: Read the entry for *momentary*. Then answer the questions. Review page 630 in your handbook if you get stuck.

> **Thesaurus Entry**
>
> **momentary,** *adj.* fleeting, quick, passing, flitting, flashing, transient, impermanent, shifting, ephemeral, vanishing, cursory, temporary, dreamlike. —**Antonyms:** eternal, continual, ceaseless.

1. What part of speech is *momentary*?

2. What are some synonyms for *momentary*?

3. What are some antonyms?

Step 2: Use the synonyms.

Using the synonyms can help you remember them.

Directions: Use synonyms for *momentary* to complete these phrases.

1. Our   wish

2. Not permanent, but

3. A   mirage

Vocabulary

Author/Title Index

Photo Credit

20 ©Bettmann/CORBIS

70 courtesy of Library of Congress

99 ©Photodisc

187 courtesy of Library of Congress